ENGLISH-SPEAKING JUSTICE

GEORGE GRANT

English-Speaking Justice

Anansi   Toronto

House of Anansi Press is grateful for the assistance of The Canada Council and the Ontario Arts Council.
Cover photograph of George Grant, courtesy of Dorothy Richardson.
Cover design: Laurel Angeloff.
Printed in the United States of America.

English-Speaking Justice is published in Canada by arrangement with the University of Notre Dame Press, Notre Dame, Indiana, by:

House of Anansi Press Limited
35 Britain Street
Toronto, Ontario M5A 1R7
Canada

Canadian Cataloguing in Publication Data

Grant, George, 1918-
    English-speaking justice

First published: Sackville, N.B. : Mount Allison University, 1974. — (The Josiah Wood lectures ; 1974)
Includes bibliographical references.
ISBN 0-88784-141-4

1. Justice - Addresses, essays, lectures.
2. Liberalism - Addresses, essays, lectures.
I. Title.

JC578.G7   1985   320'.01'1   C84-099513-X

To ALEX COLVILLE and DENNIS LEE
two artists who have taught me about justice

Introduction

English-Speaking Justice was first delivered as The Josiah Wood Lectures at Mount Allison University in 1974 and was published by the University in 1978. Anansi is pleased to co-publish the present edition with the University of Notre Dame Press. The text is essentially the same as the Mount Allison edition, except for the expansion of certain citations in the footnotes.

George Parkin Grant was born in 1918 in Toronto and studied at Upper Canada College, Queen's University and Oxford University. He has taught philosophy and religious studies at McMaster University and has been the Killam Professor at Dalhousie University. His works include *Philosophy in the Mass Age* (1959), *Lament for a Nation: The Defeat of Canadian Nationalism* (1965), *Time as History* (1969), and *Technology and Empire: Perspectives on North America* (1969). He is married, with six children, and lives in Halifax.

Josiah Wood Lectureship

The following comprises the main portion of the deed of gift from the Honourable Josiah Wood, D.C.L., dated May 28, 1925:

As we grow older there is a danger of looking back on our early days and considering them much better than the present; but even the optimistic will admit that in recent years spiritual and moral progress has not kept pace with material advancement.

Since the infirmities of my advancing years have obliged me to live retired at my home in Sackville, and I have been largely confined to the house, with leisure to read the paper, I have been surprised at the wrong-doing and crimes that have been almost daily recorded in them. I have been impressed with the fact that the stern integrity of our fathers has been gradually weakened, and in many cases has entirely disappeared. Occupations and pleasures which, in their days, would have been regarded as wrong are without hesitation indulged in. In business, profit is the first consideration, and little thought is given to the moral character of the transactions. Indeed, wilful fraud and deliberate crime have been frequently discovered and exposed.

When I was a member of the Canadian Senate I did not draw all the money to which I was legally entitled.

I did not then intend that it should be taken from the public treasury. During my retirement, however, I have felt a desire to do something with this money which would have a tendency to lessen evil, and to benefit society generally. In this way it seemed possible to make this money practically useful. Upon mature reflection it has appeared to me that to establish a foundation for a lecture course in connection with Mount Allison University at Sackville will meet my views. The principal is to be invested and to be kept invested in securities which are at the time legal investments for trust funds in the Province of New Brunswick. The income is to be appropriated, partly as an honorarium for one or more lectures each year, and partly in the printing and distribution of the lectures. The lectures shall be delivered by men of high standing and exceptional ability. The lecturer shall be free to deal with his subject as he thinks best, keeping in mind the fundamental idea for which this foundation is established, namely, to impress on our students and citizens generally the absolute necessity of honesty and honour, of integrity and truthfulness, of an altruistic public spirit, of loyalty to King and Country and of reverence for God; in short, of all those virtues which have long been recognized as the very basis of the highest type of citizenship. I desire that a copy of the lectures be given to each student and Professor in the University and a copy be sent free to every University library in Canada. Other copies may be sold, in so far as there is a demand for them.

My desire is to assist in carrying out the purpose which the late Charles F. Allison had in mind in founding an Educational Institution in Sackville. These lectures are, therefore, always to be delivered in connection with the Foundation there bearing his name. The President of the University with the Treasurer of the Board of Regents and one other appointed each year by the Regents shall be trustees who will be responsible for arranging the lectures year by year and carrying out the terms of this bequest. This trust shall be know as the Josiah Wood Lectureship.

Part I

During this century western civilisation has speeded its world-wide influence through the universal acceptance of its technology. The very platitudinous nature of this statement may hide the novelty which is spoken in it. The word 'technology' is new, and its unique bringing together of 'techne' and 'logos' shows that what is common around the world is this novel interpenetration of the arts and sciences. As in all marriages, this new union of making and knowing has changed both parties, so that when we speak 'technology' we are speaking a new activity which western Europeans brought into the world, and which has given them their universalising and homogenising influence. Kant's dictum that 'the mind makes the object' were the words of blessing spoken at that wedding of knowing and production, and should be remembered when we contemplate what is common throughout the world.

The first task of thought in our era is to think what that technology is: to think it in its determining power over our politics and sexuality, our music and education. Moreover we are called to think that technological civilisation in relation to the eternal fire which flames forth in the Gospels and blazes even in the presence of that determining power.

We English-speakers have a particular call to contemplate this civilisation. We have been the chief practical influence in taking technology around the world. Russians and Chinese have often communicated with each other in the language of a small island off the west coast of Europe. Bismarck said that the chief fact of nineteenth century politics was that the Americans spoke English. To assert this practical influence does not imply the absurd suggestion that technological civilisation is mainly a product of the English-speaking world. Names such as Heisenberg and Einstein remind us that the crowning intellectual achievement of modernity was not accomplished by English-speakers. Descartes and Rousseau, Kant and Nietzsche, remind us that those who have thought most comprehensively about modernity have often not been English-speaking. Nevertheless, in theory and practice we English-speakers have universalised technological civilisation; we have recently established its most highly explicit presence in North America. In the very fullness of this presence we are called to think what we are.

As a small part of this multiform task, I intend in these Wood lectures to start from one fact of our situation: the close relation that there has been between the development of technology and political liberalism. By thinking about that relation, I hope to throw light on the nature of both, our liberalism and technology.

Over the last centuries, the most influential people in the English-speaking world have generally taken as their dominant form of self-definition a sustaining faith in a necessary interdependence between the developments of technological science and political liberalism. Most of our scientists have been political (and indeed moral and religious) liberals; the leading philosophic and journalistic expounders of liberalism have nearly always tied the possibility of realising a truly liberal society to the potentialities of modern mastering science. Indeed that close interdependence appears most obviously in the way that some convinced modern liberals put forth their creed as if it were a product of modern science itself; that is, speaking about it in the very language of objectivity which is appropriate to scientific discoveries, but not to an account of the political good. The expression of that close relationship has greatly varied. On the one hand there have been those who held the identification because they believed political liberalism was the best means of guaranteeing the progress of science. (Freedom's great achievement was that it allowed modern technology to appear.) On the other hand, there have been those who emphasised that modern science was a means of actualising the good which was liberal society. (Technology's great achievement was that it allowed freedom to flourish.) Whatever these differences of emphasis, however that close identification rested finally in a widely shared belief that the same account of reason which resulted in the discoveries of science, also expressed itself humanly in the development of political regimes ever more congruent with the principles of English-speaking liberalism. This assumed relation of modern science and modern liberalism is still our dominant form of public self-definition, whatever vagaries it has suffered in the twentieth century. Indeed, what do we English-speaking people possess of the political good, if we do not possess what is given in our particular liberalism?

It might be argued that I am incorrect to summon forth one side of that relation by the word 'liberalism'. It is indeed true that North American journalists often obscure practical issues by opposing 'liberalism' to 'conservatism'. A clearer way of speaking is to call the practical opposite of 'conservatism' 'progressivism'. Liberalism in its generic form is surely something that all decent men accept as good—'conservatives' included. In so far as the word 'liberalism' is used to describe the belief that political liberty is a central human good, it is difficult for me to consider as sane those who would deny that they are liberals. There can be sane argument concerning how far political liberty can be achieved in particular times and places, but not concerning whether it is a central human good. It may seem therefore that the use of the word 'liberal' about our explicit political faith during the last centuries does nothing to specify that faith clearly, other than to state the platitude that it was part of the broad tradition of sane discourse in the western world. Would it not be better to use for the purposes of general description the phrase 'English-speaking progressivism'? Despite this argument, I will use the phrase 'English-speaking liberalism', because it makes clear the two following points. First, the institutions and ideas of the English-speaking world at their best have been much more than a justification of progress in the mastery of human and non-human nature. They have affirmed that any regime to be called good, and any progress to be called good, must include political liberty and consent. It is not simply a racialist pride in our own past that allows us to make that boast. This must be reaffirmed these days, when our tradition seems often to have degenerated into an ideology the purpose of which is to justify the uninhibited progress of cybernetics, and when therefore it is very easy for decent men to attack English-speaking liberalism as a shallow ideology. Secondly, the use of the word 'liberalism' rather than 'progressivism' emphasises the necessary point that our English-speaking variety is not liberalism itself, but a particular species of it. This is often forgotten amongst us with the result that our account of liberalism is taken to be the only authentic account, rather than a particular expression of it. This arrogance has often made us depressingly provincial, especially in our philosophising.[1]

Two general propositions seem true about our contemporary liberalism. On the one hand, it is the only political language that can sound a convincing moral note in our public realms. On the other hand, there are signs that modern liberalism and technology, although they have been interdependent, may not necessarily be mutually sustaining, and that their identity may not be given in the nature of reason itself. These two propositions are fundamental to this writing.

The first appears to me indubitable. If argument is to appear respectable and convincing publicly, it must be spoken within the broad assumptions of modern liberalism. Arguments from outside this tradition are put out of court as irrational and probably reactionary. This response is so part of the air we breathe that we often forget its existence. For example, reactions against liberalism emerge on our continent based on local patriotisms and parochialities. These reactions are rarely able to sustain any national control of public policy, partially because the moral language in which they express themselves can easily be shown to be 'irrational' in terms of liberal premises, by the dominant classes of our society and their instruments of legitimation. Or again, the language of traditional religion can sustain itself in the public realm only insofar as it responds to issues on the same side as the dominating liberalism. If it does, it is allowed to express itself about social issues. But if there is a conflict between the religious voices and the liberalism, then the religious voices are condemned as reactionary and told to confine themselves to the proper place of religion, which is the private realm. It was not surprising that an influential liberal philosopher defined religion as what we do with our solitude, and in so doing turned around the classical account of religion. Or again, people who wish to justify certain moral positions are forced to pay lip service to modern liberalism if their arguments are to be convincing. The paying of lip service is always evidence of the dominance of a particular way of thought. There was a time when lip service had to be paid to Christianity. In our present world, lip service must be paid to liberalism.

For example, the bell of liberalism sounded in the fall of Nixon. The waves of public indignation which made possible his fall were too sustained to have been produced simply because the wind machines were owned by his enemies. The fact that so many had an obvious interest in bringing about his fall must not allow one to forget that they finally depended for their success on the disinterested voices of those who truly believed in the universal principles of liberal government. Indeed, the surprise in other parts of the world that the Americans were getting rid of an effective president, simply because of a few domestic crimes, showed unawareness of the strength of political liberalism in the heartland of that empire. Those who were surprised showed that they only understood the United States as an object—that is, from outside.

The reason why modern liberalism is the only language that can seem respectable in the public realm is because the dominant people in our society still take for granted that they find in it the best expression of moral truth. This must be stated unequivocally because some of us often find ourselves on the opposite side of particular issues from that espoused by the liberal majority, and do not accept the deepest premises, which undergird liberalism, concerning what human beings are. It is disturbing to find that a belief that does not appear to one rationally convincing is nevertheless the dominating belief in the world one inhabits.

If one wants to communicate, it is constantly necessary to use language which cannot express one's own grasp of reality. The escape from this can be paranoia, which expressed itself in the U.S. as the belief that the dominance of modern liberalism was produced simply by a conspiracy of 'intellectuals', 'media people', 'the eastern establishment' etc. Paranoia in any form is always the enemy of sanity and charity. This particular paranoia is especially dangerous because it closes the eyes to the essential fact that modern liberalism has been dominant because the dominant classes in our society have taken for granted that it expressed what is good. For a century the majority of people have at the centre of their education received the belief that the modern liberal account of justice is the best account. To accept the implications of the fact is a 'sine qua non' of any sane vision of English-speaking societies.

To turn to the second proposition: it is not difficult to point to facts which suggest that technological development does not sustain political liberalism. Abroad, the tides of American corporate technology have not washed up liberal regimes on the shores of their empire. Indeed, to put it mildly, the ferocious determination of the Americans to keep Indo-China within the orbit of their empire made

clear that the rights to life, liberty and the pursuit
of happiness might be politically important for members of the domestic heartland, but were not intended
to be applicable to the tense outreaches of that empire. In the light of these facts, the argument is still
presented by liberals that unfree regimes arise in colonial areas when they are first being modernised,
but that in the long run they will develop into liberal
domocracies. By this argument the identity of technological advance and liberalism is preserved in
thought. The strength of the argument is necessarily weakened, however, as fewer and fewer colonial
regimes remain constitutional democracies. The
question is then whether the argument is an appeal
to progressivist hope, or to facts; or whether progressivist faith is indeed fact.[2]

However, it is in the heartlands of the English-
speaking empire that the more fundamental facts appear which put in question the mutual interdependence of technological and liberal reason. The chief
of these facts is that the development of technology
is now increasingly directed towards the mastery of
human beings. In the words of Heidegger, the sciences are now organised around cybernetics—the
technology of the helmsman. To state part of what
is given in that thought: technology organises a
system which requires a massive apparatus of ar-
tisans concerned with the control of human beings.
Such work as behaviour modification, genetic engineering, population control by abortion are ex-
treme examples. The machinery reaches out to control more and more lives through this apparatus, and

its alliance with the private and public corporations necessary to technological efficiency. The practical question is whether a society in which technology must be oriented to cybernetics can maintain the institutions of free politics and the protection by law of the rights of the individual. Behind that lies the theoretical question about modern liberalism itself. What were the modern assumptions which at one and the same time exalted human freedom and encouraged that cybernetic mastery which now threatens freedom?

Moreover, what can be the place of representative government in the immense society ruled by private and public corporations with their complex bureaucracies?[3] The great founders of our liberalism believed that the best regime required that the choices of all its members should have influence in the governing of the society. It was also hoped that free and equal individuality would be expressed in our work as a field for our choices. The free society would require the overcoming of the division of labour, so that our individuality could be expressed in an egalitarian variety of work. How are either of these possible when the dominant decisions come forth from private and public corporations? In this situation, the institutions of representative government seem increasingly to wither in their effectiveness. Lip service is paid to them; but institutions such as elections and parliaments seem to have less and less constitutive authority. The work of most human beings is intensely specialised, and proceeds from routines which have little to do with individual spontaneity. The widespread concentration of most North Americans on private life, and their acceptance that the public realm is something external to them, takes us far away from the original liberal picture of autonomous and equal human beings participating in the government and production of their society.

Indeed, the current concentration on private life, and the retreat from the public realm as something which is other, raises questions beyond the practical failures of our liberalism. It raises fundamental questions about what is being spoken about human beings in that liberalism. Its theoretical founders asserted that justice was neither a natural nor supernatural virtue, but arose from the calculations necessary to our acceptance of the social contract. In choosing the benefits of membership in organised society, we choose to obey the contractual rules of justice. But is not the present retreat into the private realm not only a recognition of the impotence of the individual, but also a desire to leave the aridity of a realm where all relations are contractual, and to seek the comfort of the private where the supracontractual is possible? For example, the contemporary insistence on sexual life as the chief palliative of our existence is clearly more than a proper acceptance of sexuality after nineteenth century repressions. It is also a hunger and thirst for ecstatic relations which transcend the contractual. After all, mutual orgasmic intercourse cannot finally be brought under the rules of contract, because it takes one beyond the realm of bargains. Therefore human beings rely on its immediacy partially as a retreat from the arid world of public contractualism. In this sense, the retirement of many from the public realm raises deeper questions about modern liberalism than its practical failure to achieve its ideals. It raises questions about the heart of liberalism: whether the omnipresence of contract in the public realm produces a world so arid that most human beings are unable to inhabit it, except for dashes into it followed by dashes out. But such a tenuous relation to the public realm is far from the intentions of the early founders of modern liberalism. This leads to asking: was the affirmation by those founders that justice is based on contract ever sufficient to support a politics of consent and justice? This questions modern liberalism at its theoretical heart.

To sum up: we are faced by two basic facts about our moral tradition. First, our liberalism is the only form of political thought which can summon forth widespread public action for the purposes of human good. Secondly, this liberalism seems presently to speak with a confused voice in the face of the technology it has encouraged and this confusion puts in question the theoretical roots of that liberalism. These lectures will, therefore, try to enucleate what is being spoken about human and non-human beings in that liberal tradition. Only in the light of such an enucleation can one turn to the more difficult question of what is the relation between technological reason and modern liberal reason.

Part II

What is being spoken about human beings in our contemporary liberalism now that technology is not simply a dreamed hope but a realising actuality? I will seek this by discussing a recent writing: *A Theory of Justice*, by Professor John Rawls of Harvard. The centre of the English-speaking world has moved since 1914 to the great republic. It is therefore appropriate to listen to contemporary liberalism in an American garb. Harvard has been an intellectual centre of that empire. Since President Eliot, the ends of that university have more and more seemed to be the stamping of liberal ideology on the articulate classes of that empire. A book of six hundred pages about justice is a good place to start. Justice is after all the central political question and a carefully composed theory of it, clearly within contemporary liberal assumptions, allows us to hear much of what is being spoken about human beings in that liberalism.[4]

Rawls affirms that justice can only be truly understood when it is known as rooted in contract. He summons forth as his chief teachers the great contractarian theorists of modern liberalism, Locke,

Rousseau, Kant; he sees his task as expressing their fundamental contractarian truth in terms which will be acceptable to contemporary analytical philsophising. Indeed among those who have written about political liberalism in the English-speaking world there have been two main conceptual schemes: those who have been purely utilitarian and those who have subordinated utilitarianism within a firm contractarian frame. Rawls places his liberalism within such a frame and his book is a sustained criticism of pure utilitarianism as the basis for a free society. It is surely not hard to understand that contractarian theory has always protected the rights of individuals in a way that utilitarian theory does not allow, and that this is a pressing issue at a time such as ours when the rights of individuals are assailed by progressive corporate power, acting under the banner of technological necessities. In terms of utilitarianism's own first principle, why should individuals have inalienable rights, if those rights stand in the way of the greatest happiness of the greatest number? When applied to the actual world of politics, contractarian theory has always supported a legal and political system which grasped the nitty-gritty of justice in its details, while the broad principle of utilitarianism could be used to sweep them away. It is for this reason that contractarian theorists such as Locke and Rousseau have had direct influence on actual politicians to an extent never achieved by utilitarians such as Hume and Bentham. The politicians had to come to terms with the details of justice in terms of individuals. Therefore when Rawls insists on the superiority of Locke to Hume, we seem to be entering a world which is much less flaccid about what can be done to individuals than the world called forth by successors of Hume. Can we do anything to individuals in the name of minimising the misery of the greatest number? In starting from the great contractarians, Rawls gives us hope that we will meet the complexities and difficulties of political justice in a way that is not possible under the principles of mass hedonism.

Contractarian theory may seem an abstraction of philosophers, taking us away from the common sense needs of human beings so obviously faced by the utilitarians in their principle of the greatest happiness of the greatest number. Nevertheless it is more fundamental than utilitarianism because it answers the question: Why should human beings consent to even that minimal social cooperation without which organised society cannot exist? It answers this question in terms of the interests of the free individual. 'Liber' and 'free' are after all synonymous at the literal level. Its answer is that the good society is composed of free individuals who agree to live together only on the condition that the rules of cooperation, necessary to that living together, serve the overall purposes of each member of that society. That agreement or contract, and the calculating implicit in it, is the only model of political relations adequate to autonomous adults. The state must be such that each person can freely agree to the limitations it imposes, and this will only be possible when its free, rational members know that its existence is, in the main, to their advantage. Rawls is in the central tradition of modern liberalism in that his ideal political beings are adult calculators, who freely decide that social cooperation is worthwhile <u>because it is to their</u> <u>individual advantage</u>. It is in this sense that Rawls believes that the true principles of justice depend on a social contract. He believes that if one is to push to the point of philosophic clarity the idea of justice implicit in social cooperation, the conception of social contract becomes necessary, because without the social contract it is not possible to show that the acceptance of justice is to the advantage of the freely calculating individual. The vision of society as a collection of free, calculating individuals puts his book at the heart of modern liberalism. The book is the attempt to make clear the nature of that social contract (a) in the light of the new conditions of advanced technological society and (b) in terms acceptable to modern analytical philosophers.

To explicate Rawls' account of the social contract and to see whether it provides a foundation for the principles of justice he builds upon it, it is necessary to compare Rawls' account with those of his avowed masters, Locke and Kant.[5] Locke's account of the social contract is that it is made by sensible calculating human beings, in the light of their recognition of the way things are in the state of nature. In exemplary consciousness of what he is doing, Locke follows Hobbes in substituting the state of nature for the createdness of nature as the primal truth. From this truth his understanding of politics is derived. In short, Locke's belief in contractual constitutionalism as the best regime is founded upon a new primal teaching about nature which is radically distinguished from that which had been traditional to western Europe. The Aristotelian account of nature (which had been strangely put together with the doctrine of creation in the dominant western tradition) was known by Locke to be untrue, above all because of what was given in a clear philosophic reflection about the discoveries and methods of the new sciences. (It is worth remembering that as a young man Hobbes had served as a clerk in the household of Francis Bacon.) For Locke, the Aristotelian teaching could no longer be the framework for the understanding of either the human or the non-human things. In the old view of nature, human beings were understood as directed to a highest good under which all goods could be known in a hierarchy of subordination and superordination. Our lesser goods were seen as pale participations in that highest good. To Locke, the untruth of the traditional teaching means that there is no such highest good given to human beings in their recognition of the way things are. Nevertheless the understanding of the way things are — the state of nature — remains for him the only basis from which a true account of the best political regime can be understood. Put negatively then, for Locke the great question about justice must be: how can the foundations of justice be laid when rational human beings are not given the conception of a highest good? His answer to that question is that justice is contractual, not natural. The state of nature does not provide us with the con-

ception of a highest good; but it does provide us with
knowledge of the greatest evil, and the desire to
escape that evil. The calculating individual knows
that the worst evil is death, and that although we
cannot finally escape it, we must escape as long as
we can. We must preserve ourselves—if possible
comfortably. Reflection on the state of nature makes
us recognise this given end (albeit negative) and from
it a new political teaching can be laid down. In the
social contract, we agree to government and its limitations upon us because it is to our advantage, in
the sense that it protects us from the greatest evil.
That contract is the source of our rights because we
have consented to be social only upon certain conditions, and our rights are the expressions of those
limiting conditions. All members of society are equal
in the possession of these rights, because whatever
other differences there may be between human beings, these differences are minor compared to the
equality in our fundamental position: to be rational
is to be directed by the dominating desire for comfortable preservation. Justice is those convenient arrangements agreed to by sensible men who recognise
the state of nature, and what it implies concerning
the greatest evil. Because of his bland and indirect
rhetoric, Locke was to be the chief theoretical influence on generations of English-speaking bourgeois, persuading them to give their allegiance to the
new form of liberalism. In so far as they understood
his teaching as more than immediate political pre-
scriptions, they came to recognise that in accepting

that liberalism they were giving up the doctrine of creation as the primal teaching.

To be aware of what is being spoken by Rawls about human beings, it is necessary to state where his account of the social contract differs from that of Locke. Rawls' central teaching is that the principles of justice are not self-evident to our 'common sense'; the positing of an 'original position' enables us to formulate them. The original position is an imagined situation in which an individual is asked to choose principles of justice for his society under a 'veil of ignorance'. This veil conceals from him his particular circumstances, and therefore eliminates from his choosing those motives of self-interest which otherwise would corrupt the fairness of his judgement. In the original position we all would choose fairly because we would be abstracted from knowing the detailed facts about our condition in the real world. Because we would not know who we were in detail (we might be people in the most miserable conditions) we would therefore have an interest in choosing the universal principles of our society which would be good for all its members, not simply to the advantage of some. As we choose under a veil of ignorance, we would choose principles which would be good for all, because we might be one of those to whom partial principles did not apply. Chosen from this abstracted position, the principles of justice are the basis for the constitution of any just society in any time or place. The original position is Rawls' basic theoretical teaching because from it we can derive universal principles of justice acceptable to all rational human beings. All human beings can agree to say 'yes' to a society so based, because it is the one most likely to serve their advantage.

It is important to recognise that in Rawls' account of justice as fairness human beings remain essentially calculators of their own self-interest in the original position. When Rawls speaks of human beings as rational, he means that they are able to calculate their self-interest. The calculations of our self-interest are concerned with what Rawls calls 'the primary goods'. These are those goods such as wealth, liberty, status, etc. which all sensible human beings will agree are good, however much they disagree as to what is the highest good or whether there is a highest good. Calculation concerning these goods is the central activity of the original position, because in it individuals know that they have self-interest, and know the general content of those self-interests. What they do not know is the particularities of those self-interests. They do not know their place in society e.g. wealth, skills, inclinations, ambitions, private philosophies of life, etc. Indeed the original position is made timeless and ahistorical in that it does not include knowledge of the level of technological development the particular society has reached. In two essential ways Rawls' teaching is close to that of Locke's social contract. (1) For both Rawls and Locke the primary political act from which justice is derived is an act of individualist calculation of self-interest. (2) What men primarily calculate about are those good things which lead to comfortable self-preservation.

Nevertheless Rawls' teaching differs in substance from that of Locke. 'The original position' is an abstraction from life, according to Rawls; 'the state of nature' is the way things are, according to Locke. Nobody has ever actually lived in the original position; all reflective people are aware that they could easily find themselves in Locke's state of nature, if the conventions of civil society were wiped away. What holds us in society according to Locke is our consciousness of what we have to lose (life itself) if we do not put up with the convenient rules of the game. The fear of violent death is the reason for setting up those rules and it remains the final reason for staying with them. Rawls' original position is not concerned with the way things are, it is an imagined abstraction from that. Justice is as much a matter of convenient rules of the game as it is in Locke's teaching. But the rules of the game are derived from a quite different situation from that described by Locke. They are reached from a stance set up to achieve fairness. Clearly there is a great gulf fixed between a contract for rules of the game founded on a calculation of individual self-interest which is always aware that its chief end must be self-preservation, and a contract concerning the rules of the game founded on an imagined stance abstracted from the way things are.[6]

One clear cause of this gulf between earlier contractarian teaching and that of Rawls is that Rawls defines the activity of philosophising in a quite different way from Locke and Hobbes. It is not my business here to describe the history of English-speaking philosophy in the last centuries, or its subtle copenetration with changes in the continental account of philosophy. In journalistic terms, it suffices to state that since 1900 the 'subject' has been increasingly practised in English-speaking universities within a rubric that can be crudely labelled as 'the analytical'. Rawls practises philosophy within the broad outlines of that rubric; so what he thinks he is doing is clearly differentiated from what Locke thought he was doing.[7] In the sphere of morals and politics, analytical philosophers have often expressed their teaching within the negative principle known as 'the naturalistic fallacy': that propositions concerning how human beings ought to act cannot be derived solely from factual propositions about nature. Clearly the contractarian teaching of Hobbes and Locke is an example of 'the naturalistic fallacy', because what they both say about justice is founded upon what they claim to know about the way things are. The regime founded upon the social contract is the best regime because of the way things are in the state of nature. Locke unfortunately practised philosophy before the discovery of 'the naturalistic fallacy', the divisions between 'nature' and 'freedom', between 'is' and 'ought'. Rawls is the inheritor of these later explications. According to him the principles of justice cannot be derived from such metaphysical propositions as the state of nature. To put his difference from Locke in terms of the history of ethical theory, his doctrine of the original position may then be taken as the attempt to preserve the advantages of contractarian over utilitarian foundations for liberal justice, while avoiding 'the naturalistic fallacy' (call it if you will the metaphysical foundations) upon which Locke's contractarian teaching is based.

With the division between nature and freedom, 'is' and 'ought', we enter the world of thought dominated by Kant. It is indeed appropriate that in the preface of Rawls' book we read that his theory "is highly Kantian in nature" (viii), and that in his index we find more references to Kant than to any other thinker. Kant has been the German philosopher who over long and changing generations has most sustained his influence over English-speaking academics. That influence continued even in the years since 1870 as the English and the Germans moved into increasingly explicit economic and political conflict, and their intellectual worlds became further separate. In the public world, Kant's great political teacher, Rousseau, exerted a greater influence, first through the French revolutionists, and more recently through Marxism. But it was through the thought of Kant that the tradition of continental liberalism most firmly touched our universities. Generations of professors studied and taught Kant's writings, so that his influence penetrated the form of our education. For example, when we think about the origins of the distinction between judgements of fact and of value, we are apt to impute the formulation of this assumption to the work of Max Weber. Yet not only did Weber's formulation arise from his

study of Kant, but also in our world the long influence of Kant on academic philosophers had pre-
pared the ground for the dominance of this distinction in the social sciences. What is being attacked
as 'the naturalistic fallacy' is avoided by the distinction between judgements of fact and of value.

Indeed Rawls' notion of justice as fairness seems
on first view to take us into the political world of
rational choice which was so wonderfully explicated
by Kant. The free power of human reasoning is seen
not only as overcoming the deficiencies of nature by
developing the arts and sciences, (technology), but
also as showing us, in its impartial universalising
power, why these arbitrary and deficient allocations
of nature ought not to be allowed to continue. We
not only transcend nature in our technological ability
to correct its deficiencies, but also in our moral willing which is the statement that they ought to be cor-
rected. The human species depends for its progress
not on God or nature but on its own freedom, and
the direction of that progress is determined by the
fact that we can rationally give ourselves our own
moral laws. Within this view of freedom as transcending nature, the principle of equality is extended
to realms unthought of in the earlier contractualism
of Hobbes and Locke. It becomes no longer simply
a matter of equality in legal rights, but an equality
also of goods and powers to be distributed fairly by
the rational will of the community. At the simplest
level of interpretation, the greatness of Kant's account of justice lies in his assertion that it is irrational for human beings to make favourable excep-

tions of themselves. It is irrational to ask for goods from our communities that we do not will for other people. Rawls' account of justice as fairness is obviously close to that Kantian assertion. In the immediate political scene, the equality he advocates is an equality defined in the tradition of Rousseau, not of Locke. It is an equality not only of legal rights but of substantive goods, towards which all communities ought to strive. Such an equality is considered a sane political goal, not only because the progress of technology allows us to put right the blindness and deficiencies of nature, but also because reason teaches us that these deficiencies ought not to be.

Yet despite Rawls' continuous appeals to Kant, it is a dimmed and partial Kant which emerges. Kant is quite clear why the contractually based state founded on the rights of man is the best state. The first sentence of *The Laying of the Foundations of the Metaphysics of Morals* expresses the ontological basis of that affirmation. "Es ist überall nichts in der Welt, ja überhaupt auch ausser derselben zu denken möglich was ohne Einschränkung fur gut könnte gehalten werden, als allein ein **guter Wille**." It is not pedantry which makes me write this sentence in German. The ring of its affirmation is lost in all English translations I have read or attempted. "It is impossible to conceive anything at all in the world, or even out of it, which can be taken as good without qualification, except a good will." Yes, but not quite.[8] According to Kant we can know this to be so, because as he says in *The Critique of Practical Reason*, morality is the one fact of reason. Facts are given and our rationality gives us the very form of justice for all our actions. Indeed, as justice is present to our wills in the mood of command, reason commands us to the faith that justice is what we are finally fitted for. Our other activities may be what we are fitted for under certain circumstances, but they may not be under other circumstances. Justice is always good and is the final court of appeal for the judging of the goodness of any act. In the command to be just, given us in our very reasons, we are also given the idea that being fitted belongs essentially to us. All the uncertainties about whether we are fitted for anything which arises for us from our sense of nature's arbitrariness, our knowledge of its mechanism and the relativities of our desires, are overcome in the command, beyond all bargaining, to be just. The categorical imperative presents to us good without restriction. Moreover that justice which is our good depends upon our willing of it. We are the makers of our own laws; we are the cause of the growth of justice among our species. We are not only the species whose good is justice, but also the species who are the cause of the coming to be of our own good. According to Kant, in our ability to will justly we are both timelessly rational, outside the world where everything is relatively good and where reasoning is simply calculation; we are also utterly in the world of time where we make history, where what happens matters absolutely and depends upon our autonomous willing. What it means to say that the good will is the only good without restriction is both the traditional doctrine of the timeless factuality of the moral law; but also the new idea that as makers of our own laws we are called upon to realise justice progressively in history.[9]

Kant's account of the political in his shorter writings is firmly related to the affirmation that the good will is the only good without restriction. Kant took the contractarian teaching of Hobbes and Locke which was based on the passions of nature and founded it rather on the freedom of human beings to legislate a timeless rational morality which quite transcended nature. It may be said that he sacralised the contractarian teaching. From the side of will in the phrase 'the good will', the social contract represents the consent necessary in any regime proper to human beings whose essence is their autonomous freedom. Because the highest purpose of human life is to will autonomously, the best political regime must be such as could be willed rationally by all its members. In this sense, consent becomes the very substance of the best regime. It must be a state based on 'the rights of man', that is, giving the widest possible scope to external freedom, because any limitations on external freedom stand in the way of the exercise of our autonomy. These rights must be universal throughout society, because all human beings are equal in the sense that they are all open to the highest human end of willing the moral good. Inequalities between human beings are only concerned with lesser goods, such as intellectual or ar-

tistic powers. Concerning what matters absolutely
we are all equal in the fact that the rational willing
of our duty is open to all.

From the side of good in the phrase 'the good will',
Kant's contractarian teaching leads to a sharp division between morals and politics, and therefore to
a strict limitation on the powers of the state given
in the social contract itself. Properly understood,
morality is autonomous action, the making of our
own moral laws. Indeed any action is not moral
unless it is freely legislated by an individual. Therefore the state is transgressing its proper limits when
it attempts to impose on us our moral duties. Our
autonomous choices of timeless good cannot be so
imposed. Indeed, Kant more than any other political
philosopher, lays before us that side of liberalism
which says that the state should not interfere with
the actions of its citizens, except when those actions
infringe the external freedom of other citizens. The
state is concerned with the preservation of the external freedom of all, and must leave moral freedom
to the individual. It is concerned with the relativities
of nature understood by Kant within the non-teleo-
logical and non-substantialised view of nature given
us in modern science. When in his *Perpetual Peace*
he states that the hard problem of organising a good
regime can be solved even for a race of devils, as
long as they are intelligent, he is asserting that the
state must be limited to those natural relativities, and
that the ability to calculate is an adequate account
of reason when one is concerned with those relativities. Nowhere is Kant's affirmation that the world

of nature is strickly relative more lucidly put before us than in his definition of marriage as a life-time contract for the mutual use of the genitals. But the limitations of the state to contracts concerning these relativities is necessary in order to guard the individual's willing of the timeless good, in which he quite transcends those relativities. It is on moral grounds that the morally neutral state is the best state. The state is limited in the social contract because the good will is the only good without restriction.[10]

For all Rawl's appeals to Kant, the central ontological affirmations of Kant are absent from Rawls. Clearly in Rawls' account of philosophy there can be no fact of reason. Justice, therefore, cannot be justified as coming forth from the universal morality given us in reason itself. Rawls cannot make the affirmation that the good will is the only good without restriction, or that the good will is that which wills the universal moral law. His account of philosophy does not allow him such statements about the supreme good.

What Rawls takes from Kant is partial in a way common among contemporary English-speaking teachers of philosophy. The central import of the critical system is interpreted in a way that leaves Kant essentially a precursor of modern analytical philosophy. His tribute to Hume as having awakened him from his dogmatic slumbers is emphasised; his stronger, more positive and more often repeated tributes to Rousseau seem to have been forgotten. It is only necessary to quote one of these tributes to make clear that Kant does not take as limited an account of the scope of philosophy as is usual among English-speaking academics: "Newton was the first to discern order and regularity in combination with great simplicity, where before him men had encountered disorder and unrelated diversity. Since Newton the comets follow geometric orbits. Rousseau was the first to discover beneath the varying forms human nature assumes, the deeply concealed essence of man and the hidden law in accordance with which Providence is justified by his observations."[11]

When Kant is taken as essentially a precursor of modern analytical philosophy, certain sides of his thought are being correctly grasped. Obviously he is a great philosopher of science and the greatest critic of traditional western metaphysics. There is no more wonderful account than his of the darkness in which we find ourselves when we attempt to apply the conception of final cause to the understanding of nature. Our fate is to find ourselves agnostic (in the literal sense) about the purpose of the way things are. He enucleates how that agnosticism has been presented with a new certainty to educated people through the discoveries of modern science. He is as aware as Hobbes or Locke of the consequences of the Galilean physics for our practical lives. Our knowledge of justice cannot be derived from our knowledge of nature (as some once believed) because our knowledge of nature is not teleological. Indeed Kant has as often been taken as a precursor of modern existentialism, as of modern analytical philosophy. We are thrown into a world of otherness. Yet, and it is an enormous 'yet', across the darkness of that agnosticism there is thrown, according to Kant, the beacon light of our knowledge of what is required of us concerning justice. That requirement is presented to all human beings from the earliest days of their reasoning, in the categorical commands of our reason itself. According to Kant, we are not in darkness concerning the one thing absolutely needful for us all. Because there is that beacon (the one fact of reason), Kant's purpose is not simply to criticize metaphysics as such, but out of his criticism of the traditional metaphysics to lay the foundations of the new one. As he makes consummately clear in the preface to the 2nd edition of *The Critique of Pure Reason*, metaphysics must become Rousseau's 'Socratic wisdom'. It is the laying of the metaphysical foundations necessary to protect that beacon light of justice. These protecting foundations are necessary on the one hand against the intellectual extremities of dogmatists who would deny our moral autonomy in denying our darkness; and on the other hand against the sceptics who would deny that there is this beacon light of justice. This 'Socratic wisdom' requires that we affirm statements which are 'beyond physics'—statements about God and about freedom. Clearly the proposition that the good will is the only good without restriction is an ontological proposition. To interpret Kant as if he were simply a precursor of modern analytical philosophy is to lay him upon a bed of Procrustes and cut his thought down to a required ametaphysical shape. Rawls passes beyond this in taking Kant as an ethical theorist whose love of egalitarian justice he admires. But by cutting Kant's ethics off from its ontological foundations, he nevertheless proceeds to the work of Procrustes upon that analytical bed.

Rawls' difference from Kant is seen in his account of 'the free and rational person'. According to Rawls, rationality is analytical instrumentality; freedom means that we cannot avoid choices. This is different from Kant's account of our free moral self-legislation as participation in the very form of reason itself. This difference becomes obvious when it is cashed in political effect around the question of equality. Why is it good that all human beings should live in a society to which they can give consent and in which they are guaranteed an equality of political liberties? Why is it good that human beings should have political rights of a quite different order from members of the other species? Why should equality in legal rights stand above and not be influenced by the obvious inequalities in contribution to progress whether in production, in the arts or in the sciences? To Kant, the answer is quite clear. The only good without restriction is the good will, and that is open to all human beings irrespective of their other differences. Our differences in talent, in education and social contribution count as nothing against fundamental equality, because we are equal in what is essential. In our moral willing we take part in the very form of reason itself. But why does Rawls' account of the 'person' make equality our due? Why are beings who can calculate and cannot avoid choices worthy of equal inalienable rights? After all, some humans can calculate better than others. Why then should they not have fuller legal rights than the poor calculators? Why do either of these human abilities justify the primacy of equality, or the different level of our rights compared with those of other species?

Nor can it be said that Rawls' use of the word 'person' illuminates his position. Indeed his use of the word seems at odds with his analytical account of philosophy. To call human beings 'persons' is clearly not a scientific description. What is it then? If the word is a true description but not scientific, is it not then one of these supra-scientific metaphysical terms which analytical philosophy would have us eschew? One may be glad that Rawls has inherited the noble belief in political equality, and the belief that 'the free and rational person' is 'valuable' in a way quite different from members of other species. But in an era such as ours, we cannot help hoping that he will tell us why it is so. His writing is typical of much modern liberal thought in that the word 'person' is brought in mysteriously (one might better say sentimentally) to cover up the inability to state clearly what it is about human beings which makes them worthy of high political respect. Where Kant is clear concerning this, Rawls is not.

In short, Rawls affirms a contractarian as against a utilitarian account of justice, but wishes to free that contractarian teaching from the metaphysical assumptions upon which it was founded in the thought of its greatest exponents. To state how successful he is in this attempt, it is necessary to return to Rawls' account of how the question of justice arises, and how his teaching concerning 'the original position' claims to answer it.

According to Rawls, the question of justice arises because all sensible people know that they have interests, and also know that these interests are sometimes going to be in conflict with those of other people. They also know that it is in their interest to live in organised society, not only to protect themselves in the pursuit of their interests against others who may interfere with such pursuits, but also positively to further their particular interests through such means as the division of labour.[12] In the light of this plurality of interests and the plurality of opinion as to what is good, how can we come to agreement about foundational rules for the social system? These foundations must reconcile the need to live in society with the need to pursue our own interests. Such basic rules are what Rawls means by the principles of justice. They are the basis of any decent constitution. Through the constitution they set the limits to positive laws, and therefore the limits within which all public relationships should take place. This account of the political situation in which the question of justice arises in terms of essentially calculating individuals may be described accurately as American bourgeois common sense. So to describe it is not meant simply derisively. It would be foolish to deride the American bourgeois self-image because it has become dominant in most of the western world, and views do not become widely dominant without at least some partial sense in them.

How are we to come to knowledge of such basic rules? Let us imagine, says Rawls, an original position in which human beings are under a veil of ignorance, so that they know that they have interests, and know that these interests are likely to be in conflict with those of other people, but do not know their own particular ones. In such a position, human beings who calculate sensibly would choose a society in which "each person is to have an equal right to the most extensive basic liberty compatible with a similar liberty for others." Rawls' first principle of justice is identical with J.S. Mill's sole principle. Sensible human beings would choose a society founded on such a principle, because under a veil of ignorance they would calculate that such a fundamental rule would allow them to pursue their own interests at least partially. Without such a rule they would chance finding themselves in a situation where they might even be unable to pursue their interests at all. For example, they might be enslaved. From the original position we reach therefore a universal principle of justice. It is universal in that it would be chosen by any sensibly calculating individual if he were in the position of calculating about interests in the abstract; that is, calculating as if he were everybody, and not simply himself or herself. This abstracted calculation is able to provide the universal principle of justice because it is a calculation about calculating which would be made by all good calculators. To repeat, human beings for Rawls are, in their public role, calculators of their interests. The act of thought in the original position might be called disinterested calculation because it is made outside any knowledge of particular interests; it is not disinterested, however, in that the calculation of interest in general is its very centre. Substantively it provides a first principle of justice because it comes to terms with the basic difficulty of any political thought. It shows how consent can be reconciled with the necessity for organised society. Consent is only possible when we know that the society is organised for the pursuit of individual interests in general.

It is important to emphasise that this account of the derivation of the first principle of justice appears to Rawls to have the enormous advantage of not requiring any knowledge of the way things are beyond common sense. It does not depend on our being able to attain any knowledge of what human beings are fitted for. Our legal rights, so derived from the original position, in no way depend on any public affirmations concerning what is good. Indeed it would appear that according to Rawls enlightened human beings are quite clear that it is not possible to have knowledge of the highest good. But if many citizens (perhaps even the majority) misguidedly think such knowledge possible, this opinion need not affect the morally neutral state, because its principles of justice can be clearly determined quite outside any opinions concerning that possibility. Indeed the doctrine of the original position claims that at one and the same time it preserves the state as morally neutral, yet also guarantees that such a state protects the rights of free and equal citizens. Moral pluralism about 'life-plans' is guaranteed by the law so long as those plans do not harm other people or interfere with their basic liberties. We are thus freed from the bad old days when the powers of the state were used to enforce the monistic opinions of some concerning goodness, on the unwilling lives of others. We are able to achieve this tolerance without sacrificing our certainty about the superior justice of the liberal regime. Moreover in terms of modern theory the chief advantage of the original position is that it enables us to free ourselves from all the difficulties and disagreements of the traditional political philosophy, which arose from its dependence on metaphysical assumptions. We free ourselves from that burden of speculation while remaining quite certain about the principles of political justice. Philosophy or religion become comparable to the question of sexual habit. They are simply a matter of private pursuit, unless their conclusions interfere with the liberty of others. We can think what we like metaphysically or religiously (if we have a taste for that kind of thing) as long as we recognise that these thoughts are our private business, and must have no influence in the world of the state. Philosophy and religion can be allowed to be perfectly free because their conclusions are perfectly private. On the other side of the same coin, the principles of justice so derived will remain utterly impervious to anything we know through scientific discovery. Let us say we reach the conclusion, because of the discoveries of modern science, that human beings are accidental occurrences which have arisen in a world which is completely explainable in terms of necessity and

chance. This gives us no reason to doubt that all
human beings should have the free and equal rights
of the liberal regime. As the principles of that regime
are derived solely from abstracted calculation about
obvious human interests, they will stand as self-
evidently true, however the world be explained, or
whatever it be.

Rawls derives much more than the regime of
political rights from the 'original position'. Justice
requires a regime which pursues equality in all
aspects of life, social and economic as well as
political. He shows this in terms of what he calls
'primary goods', and our calculation about them in
the original position. Primary goods are those goods
which any sensible person will know he will need,
whatever may be his particular 'life-plan'. To repeat,
according to Rawls we cannot know what is the
highest good for human beings, or whether there is
such. Nevertheless all sensible persons know that certain goods are necessary to any way to life. At an
obvious level, these are such things as food, shelter
and safety. Rawls, however, adds a long list of liberties and powers beyond these immediacies, stretching
from civil liberties all the way to the provision of
self-respect. Under the veil of ignorance in the original position, the calculating individual is not ig-
norant of the fact that he needs as much as possible
of these primary goods. He also knows that there
are unlikely to be enough of them to go around.
What he does not know is the details of his particular
possession of those goods. Neither does he know the
stage of technological development in his particular

society. In this partial ignorance, therefore, the calculating individual decides for a system which strives toward equality in these primary goods. This is a rational calculation because if he were to choose any other regime he would be likely to find himself in a position where he got less rather than more of the pie. Indeed, in certain stages of technological development, if he did not so choose he would be likely to find himself without even a sufficiency. From this rational calculation under the veil of ignorance we reach his second principle of justice. "Social and economic inequalities are to be arranged so that they are both: (a) to the greatest benefit to the least advantaged, — and (b) attached to offices and positions open to all under conditions of fair equality of opportunity."[13]

In making substantive equality necessary to the content of justice in his second principle, Rawls passes beyond the bourgeois political common sense of his first principle to what may be called American progressivist common sense. In practical terms, what he is saying is that the works of F.D. Roosevelt must be carried to their completion, probably by the Democratic party. Welfare egalitarianism can be united with the individualist pluralism of the constitution in an advanced technological society. The difficulties between liberty and equality raised by de Tocqueville must be overcome; justice requires the union of equality and liberty. Although this progressivism has its own American style, it finds its justification in European philosophy. Nature does not supply fairly. The arbitrary deficiencies of nature

and society are to be overcome in history in the name
of equality. The very definition of history as progress is the coming to be of equality. This philosophic liberalism reached its apogee in Marx. Technology and equality go so closely together as almost
to be considered one. It must be said that Rawls
takes only partially this European progressivism,
because he is always attempting to unite it with
bourgeois common sense. This can be seen in the
limits he puts on substantive equality compared with
Marxism in its originating form. At the centre of
Marxism is the belief that the realisation of equality will require such a prodigious event as the overcoming of the division of labour. This kind of question is just not present for Rawls. His acceptance
of progress as equality is restrained from that hope
by his bourgeois common sense. To put it crudely,
the overcoming of the division of labour is not likely
to be within the imaginative limits of the Harvard
professor. Substantive equality yes, but only at the
level of consumption and welfare.

Indeed what makes Rawls' book worthy of study
is that it is so typical of current liberalism in both
the intellectual and practical English-speaking
worlds. His book combines a theory of justice with
an account of the substance of justice. His theory
of justice attempts to come to terms with the intellectual difficulties which analytical philosophy has
brought against any theory of justice which transcends the analytical. His account of the substance
of justice puts together the claims of bourgeois individualism and progressive equality, typical of of-

ficial American liberalism. This strange mixture has only lately begun to be faced by its contradictions, both from the 'left' and the 'right'. However, his book is a confident exemplar of what has been the dominant moral strain in our politics.

In terms of what is happening in advanced societies, it is indeed not difficult to ridicule Rawls' hopes concerning this union of individualism and egalitarianism. The contradictions in this union have been made explicit both by 'the left' and 'the right'. Rawls' account of justice seems simply to abstract from the fact that liberty and equality now have to be realised in a society largely shaped politically by the cooperation between massive private corporations and the public corporation which coordinates their welfare. Indeed his thought seems to abstract from the very existence of these dominating powers. Can his calculating individualism bring forth a doctrine of the common good strong enough to control the ambitions of these mammoths? Can the calculating individual be a citizen in such a world, or does this account of human beings only lead to individuals concerned with consumption — above all entertainment and the orgasm as consumption?

1. critique

Even more surprising than Rawls' lack of interest in such powers within his own country is his abstraction from their influence in the world as a whole. That is, his theory of justice is written in abstraction from the facts of war and imperialism. He only deals with war around the question of the right of the individual to refuse the claims of the state. The abstraction from the facts of war and imperialism

2. critique

is particularly emptying when one remembers that
the modern liberal English-speaking regimes have
both been great imperial powers. Moreover, his
book was written during the period when his country was embarked on a savage imperial adventure
carried out under the regimes of Kennedy and Johnson, who advocated domestically the same welfare
equality and individualism which he is advocating.
Indeed his abstraction is even more surprising when
one remembers that the Vietnam war was justified
in terms of liberal ideology, was largely planned by
men from the liberal universities, the most influential of whom were from Rawls' own university.
Paradoxically, however, Rawls' abstraction from
war and imperialism makes his work even more
typical of our liberalism. Most American liberals
have discussed the questions of world order under
the rubric of internationalism and the relation between equal sovereign states, when in fact they lived
at the centre of a great empire. After all, that arche-
type of modern liberalism, F. D. Roosevelt, used
forceful language against war and imperialism at the
very time when he was consolidating an empire. Be
that as it may, Rawls' theory of justice is enormously
weakened by his failure to relate it to the facts of
imperialism or of domestic corporate power.

Such criticisms of Rawls concerning his apprehen-
sion of the technological society must not, however,
divert us from the fundamental question about his
theory. This question is the following: can the content of justice he advocates be derived from his contractual theory? He advocates many liberties and

equalities as the necessary content of a just regime. Sensible people can disagree with Rawls about the details of these liberties and equalities; but surely any decent human being will agree that liberty and equality are at the heart of political justice. Any English-speaker who cares about our tradition must be glad that our regimes have, at their best, attempted to realise such justice. But Rawls' book claims to be more than a catechism of such goods; it claims to be a theory of justice. That is, it claims to be giving us knowledge of what justice is, and how we know that a regime of liberty and equality is its core. He meets the demands of that claim by stating that we will know what justice is and why liberty and equality are necessary to it when we think the calculation of everybody's self-interest in general, abstracted from any self-interest in particular. The fundamental question about Rawls' book is whether such justice can be derived from calculation of self-interest in general.

Rawls characterises his account of justice as 'justice as fairness'. Sometimes in the reading of this long and complex book it may seem that we are being asked to play the old shell game. When we look for the bean of justice under the shell of self-interest, it has moved under the shell of altruism, and vice versa. Nevertheless when we are really able to pay attention to the mover's hands, we find that the bean is always under one shell — the shell of self-interest. Justice as fairness is under it. Justice is derived from calculation about self-interest in general. The fundamental question about Rawls' book is then whether justice as fairness can be so derived. Is it possible to believe that the complex apparatus necessary to preserving and extending liberty and equality in the midst of the technological society can be known as necessary to the best regime simply by thinking through the calculation of self-interest in general?

It must be insisted (yet once again) that this calculation is carried out within a particular account of what we can know about self-interest. Indeed, Plato's account of justice might be sensibly described as known by a calculation concerning self-interest. When Socrates tells us that it is better to suffer injustice than to inflict it, he is saying that it is always in our interest to be just. But in his account our interests are known through our knowledge of the nature of things. Justice is what we are fitted for. We come to know that through the practice of philosophy, which gives us knowledge of the nature of things, of what we are fitted for and what the consequences are for our actions in being so fitted. In philosophy we are given sufficient knowledge of the whole of the nature of things to know what our interests are, and to know them in a scheme of subordination and superordination. In this account, justice is not a certain set of external political arrangements which are a useful means of the realisation of our self-interests; it is the very inward harmony of human beings in terms of which they are alone able to calculate their self-interest properly. The outward regime mirrors what is inward among the dominant people of that regime, and vice versa. Within that

account, justice could then be described as the calculation of self-interest, as long as it is understood
that at the centre of that self-interest is justice itself.
For justice is the inward harmony which makes a
self truly a self (or in more accurate language which
today sounds archaic: Justice in its inward appearance is the harmony which makes a soul truly
a soul).

Obviously Rawls means something very different
by the calculation of self-interest. His analytical account of philosophy does not allow him to think that
our knowledge of self-interest can be derived from
what knowledge we have of the way things are as
a whole. Such knowledge is not possible according
to his account of philosophy. Nor (as has been
argued previously) can analytical philosophy allow
him even that knowledge of self interest which Locke
claims can be derived from our knowledge of the
nature of things as a whole. According to Locke,
we can place self-interest in an order of subordination and superordination, because our knowledge
of the way things are as a whole (the state of nature)
tells us that everybody's chief interest is the avoidance
of violent death. Justice is derived from that knowledge of our highest self-interest.[14] For Rawls the
calculated self-interest in general is not derived from
any such knowledge. It is avowedly not derived from
any contemporary philosophic or scientific knowledge. Our self-interests are "the primary goods", and
these are simply accepted as obviously our interest,
whatever may be the nature of things as a whole.
Indeed, much of Rawls' book is taken up with show-

ing the superiority of his contractarianism to utilitarianism. Nevertheless his account of 'primary
goods' is hard to distinguish from the utilitarian account of pleasure. As far as the calculation of the
political contract is concerned, self-interest in general
is the maximising of the cosy pleasures. It is taken
as self-evident that this is everybody's self-interest,
irrespective of what anybody may claim to know
about the way things are as a whole. I do not imply
that there is anything bad about cosy pleasures.
Much of our life is concerned with them. The point
is, however, that Rawls derives justice from a
calculation which is in terms of them alone. What
kind of regime will result?

What must be asked then about Rawls' theory is
not only whether justice as liberty and equality can
arise from a social contract reached from a calculation of self-interest in general; but also whether it
can be derived from a calculation in which the interests are self-evidently independent of any account
of the way things are as a whole. After all, the first
question has been on the agenda of political philosophy since our contractarian theory was first enucleated by Hobbes and Locke: is justice simply pursued because we calculate that it is the most convenient means to our self-interest? Rawls raises nothing
new about that question. What he adds, however,
is the attempt to justify this contractarianism within
analytical assumptions: Is justice pursued because
of convenience, even when the calculation is in terms
of an account of self-interest reached in abstraction
from any knowledge of the way things are as a

whole? Is such justification of justice able to support the pursuit of liberty and equality at a time when the conveniences of technology do not seem to favour them?

It may be argued that I have made too much of one academic book. One swallow does not make a summer; one academic book does not make an autumn of our justice. However, theories are at work in the decisions of the world, and we had better understand them.

Part III

Why is it that liberalism remains the dominating political morality of the English-speaking world, and yet is so little sustained by any foundational affirmations? At the level of immediate historical cause, this is not difficult to understand. The long ascendency of English-speaking peoples, in the case of England since Waterloo, and the United States since 1914, was achieved under the rule of various species of bourgeois. Members of classes are liable to consider their shared conceptions of political goodness to be self-evident when their rule is not seriously questioned at home, and when they are successfully extending their empires around the world. Those shared conceptions of constitutional liberalism seemed to be at one with technological progress, particularly as this progress was being achieved above all by English-speakers. This unity between progress in liberty and in technology, under English-speaking guidance, was often further guaranteed by being enfolded in such doctrines as the ascent of man.

In the case of England, the victory of the Whigs in 1688, and the almost unopposed consolidation of that victory after 1715, provided the political and ideological setting for the development of the first industrial society with its maritime empire. English constitutional liberalism was immensely flexible under Whig guidance. As new bourgeois classes appeared in the quick changes of a technological society, they were allowed near power, and persuaded to loyalty to the Whig constitution. The constancy among the articulate classes concerning what constituted the best regime was such that there was little need to wonder as to what was being said about human and non-human nature in the foundations of that liberalism. It was so assumed and so successful that it did not need to be thought.

In that bourgeois dominance the notes of comfort, utility and mastery could alone ring fully in the public realm. Among those who wrote political philosophy since Hobbes and Locke, there has been little more than the working out in detail of variations on utilitarianism and contractualism, their possible conflicts and their possible internal unclarities. What do Bentham or J. S. Mill or Russell add to Locke at the level of fundamental political theory? Indeed it is better to put the question: what has been lost in them of his comprehensiveness, subtlety and depth? The confidence of that Whig dominance is illustrated by the way that Burke has been interpreted since his day. He has been taken as our chief 'conservative' in contradistinction of our 'liberals'. In fact he was in practice a Rockingham Whig, and did not depart from Locke in fundamental matters, except to surround his liberalism with a touch of romanticism. That touch of the historical sense makes him in fact more modern than the pure milk of bourgeois liberalism. Such figures as Swift and Johnson and Coleridge, who attempted (in descending order of power) to think of politics outside the contractarian or utilitarian contexts, were simply taken as oddities dominated by nostalgia for a dying Anglicanism, and having no significance for the practical world.

This great confidence in bourgeois liberalism explains why the new continental philosophies of politics, from later stages of the age of progress, never seem to have exerted much influence in English intellectual life. Rousseau's account of contractarianism, based on freedom, which dominated Europe through the work of Kant and Hegel and Marx, only touched English thought in an academic way. What influential English thinker has ever come to terms with Rousseau's fundamental criticism of Hobbes and Locke? Indeed, till recently, Marxism has had little influence in England, even among the abused proletariat of the first industrial society. Since this European liberalism of freedom little penetrated English thought, it is not surprising that English thinkers hardly recognised at all the attack on that liberalism of freedom which arose in Germany. Nietzsche was not taken by the English as the great critic of Rousseau's politics, but as an obscurantist pseudo-poet. They did not need to look at his lucid analysis of what we were being told about human and non-human beings in the advancing technological society. Both for good and ill, the English thinkers were sheltered from the extremities of European political thought because of their successes under bourgeois constitutional liberalism. This was for good because the pursuit of comfortable self-preservation, though not the highest end, is certainly more decent and moderate than the extremities of communism or national socialism. There are worse things than a nation of shopkeepers. This sheltered confidence had the ill effect of leaving English intellectuals singularly unprepared to understand the extremities of the twentieth century, particularly because it had weakened the theoretical tradition in its cosy embrace.

Indeed English political philosophy has been little more than a praise of the fundamental lineaments of their own society, spiced by calls for particular reforms within those lineaments. Thinkers such as Mill or Russell were too much at home in their world to be political philosophers in the classical meaning of that term, which always implied that qua philosophers, they transcended the opinions common to their society. Even the philosophic radicals had drawing rooms. As late as our generation, after the results of two world wars had sapped the confidence of many Englishmen, and when the possibilities of technological tyranny had become obvious, the most popular academic theorising about politics went no farther than the decent prescription that we ought to pursue 'piecemeal social engineering' so as to 'minimise misery'. The only purpose of political philosophy was the valid negative task of freeing us from the delusions of general statements which might encourage a more than piecemeal engineering. Our tradition of justice was so blandly self-evident as to be in no need of further justification.

It must be insisted, however, that this long consensus about political good, and the resulting poverty of thought, did much to innoculate the English from those theoretical viruses which have plagued continental Europeans. The very weakness of philosophical life protected them from its modern extremities. The fact that the English received modern political thought in an early form from Hobbes and Locke, and continued to be generally content with that form, meant that they were free from the much more explicit modernity which arose first in France and later in Germany. Their very confidence in their liberalism saved them from taking seriously the traditions which proceeded either from Rousseau or from Nietzsche. They were for example saved from such a manifestation of those political philosophies as ideology. Clearly one of the uniquely modern phenomena has been ideologies, either of the 'left' or of the 'right'. Ideology is here defined as surrogate religion masquerading as philosophy. All forms of it have been destructive of social moderation. Its modern appearance has been chiefly caused by confusion concerning the related but distinct roles which religion and philosophy play in good societies. This confusion originated above all in the false formulation of these roles made during the French and German enlightenments. The fact that the dominant English political philosophy came from a period before those enlightenments has helped till recently in insulating the English from this virus. As illustration, the greater prestige given to scholars and artists in the German world has often resulted in an ideological politics in that country. Hitler was after all an ideologue who conceived himself as the artist in politics. The very disinterest in philosophy among the English has saved them in the past from that lack of moderation which is inherent in modern political philosophy and technology.[15]

To rise above the scholars, Churchill's writings may be taken as an example of this confidence in liberalism which did not need thought, even at a late date in that British destiny. After 1945 he wrote *A History of the English-speaking Peoples*. Here we might expect to find English liberalism lying before us as 'monumental history'. We might even expect to find a Thucydidean telling of why the deeds of those whom he had loved and to whom he had belonged had been both great and good. We might expect a telling freed from that attenuated ignorance of the heat of practice, so common in academic history. Churchill, like Bertrand Russell, came from one of the great landed families who in their rule of England and its imperial expansion had been responsible, more than any other class, for the incarnation of modern principles of liberty into the English constitution. His class had believed profoundly in the inter-dependence of commerce, domestic liberty and scientific progress. Indeed in Churchill's life of his founding ancestors, both the man and the woman, he had shown them to be substantially responsible for the origins of that Whig rule. He was a modern liberal in the sense that in domestic politics he had been an enthusiastic member of that Liberal government which first brought nationalism, social welfare and democracy together. He was a liberal in that he always maintained that superior contempt for the traditional religion, except as a useful political tool in times of emergency.[16] Churchill has often been described as a conservative, but he was only that because he appeared at a time of conflict, when his nation's constitutionalism was threatened by new alternatives — Marxist communism and national socialism. His intransigent opposition to these alternatives was expressed not only in writing but in war. Indeed he showed himself more than an English nationalist in that he believed that the American experiment was the authentic continuation of English liberalism, and was willing to sacrifice much of his country's greatness to guarantee that the torch of world leadership should be passed in our era to the capitalist republic.

One might therefore expect Churchill to state in such a late writing what it was about English-speaking liberalism which had made it worthy of loyalty such as his. One could expect an account of substantive loyalties to community goods, which is indeed not philosophy, but the only soil out of which political philosophy can arise. Such accounts carry in themselves an incipient recognition of what is said in philosophy. Particularly at that late date, one might have expected from Churchill such 'monumental history', when the ambiguity of his career must have lain before him. His career had been given to the perpetuation of English power, and yet had led to the decline of that power. However, a presentation of these loyalties in their substance and meaning is quite absent from his book. English-speaking institutions are glorified in the description of deeds, but we are not given the substance of those deeds which made them both great and loveable, other than they just happen to have been our own. Indeed the pure distance in Churchill's book between his account of action, and what good was being lived and thought in those actions, is seen in the fact that Locke is mentioned only once in the book, and then because of his work on the reformation of the coinage. The most influential thinker of the good of capitalist liberalism is not understood in relation to the deeds of that liberalism, but simply as one of those academics with which influential families decorate their lives. It seems indeed that Churchill's book is finally an appeal to pure racial will. However, such a reading would be unfair, because his failure to present good does not come from crude arbitrariness of will. He was no existentialist, but a gentleman whose loyalties transcended will. Rather it is the givenness and certainty of his loyalties which does not allow him to present those goods. Even as late as 1945, his confidence in English political greatness, and in the obvious truth of the superiority of constitutional liberalism, so enfolds him that there is no need to articulate what is good and great in the deeds he is describing.

The leading makers of the American constitution conceived themselves as influenced by political philosophy, which they took in its modern form. The

love of English political philosophy among the
French of the enlightenment came back into English-
speaking explicitness among the lawyers and intellectuals of the new world, rather than among the more
rooted English rulers. The legal and political forms
of the U.S. are more purely founded on constitutional contractualism than those of the country
where that modernism was first thought comprehensively. The pioneering expansion into an unexploited
continent gave American liberalism a greater egalitarian tint than in England. However, the coin-
cidence of that expansion with the development of
increasingly powerful forms of industrial capitalism
always resulted in these egalitarian influences being
safely confined within the practical and ideological
bounds of a given bourgeois liberalism. The egalitarianism of Paine and the egalitarianism of populism
were always subsidiary. Indeed, political contractualism and its resultant private pluralism fitted the
long term public needs of the later immigrants of
non-English traditions. The very pressures of pluralism have encouraged that interpretation of their constitution which would see it as a sheerly contractual
document. Issues in the political realm could be
decided in terms of the contracted constitutional
rights of individuals, while the denser loyalties of
existence were left supposedly untouched within
pluralism. The ideology of pluralism suited both the
institutions of industrial capitalism and the immigrant groups. It helped both the unrestrained
monistic power of the corporations, and at the same
time the entrance of members of many races (at least

those of European origin) into the freedom of the common heritage, seemingly without losing their private traditions. Increasingly, the substance of the common good was expressed rationally only as contractual reason, to the exclusion of those loyalties which gave content to that good in more traditional societies. American nationalism, with effective sense of a righteous destiny, has had to be explicitly affirmed so as to provide for the conception of the common good a substance which transcended the simply contractual. Contractualism was less inhibited even than in capitalist England, where certain disappearing classes maintained remnental reverences from before the age of progress. In the United States such remnants as Anglican poetry and piety were largely squashed with the revolution, and reverences brought by later immigrants were easily engulfed and legitimised into the public contractual framework. The crossing of the Atlantic to a society which had no history of its own from before the age of progress brought a flowering of the contractual principle in its purest form.

In the first half of this century the expansion of the United States around the world, as the great capitalist empire, was so fast and successful that the constitutional principles of bourgeois hegemony became even more self-evident.[17] Even more than in the case of England, the domestic and foreign successes of their system put contractualism safely beyond any serious thought. However much Americans have been impregnated by modern negations in other spheres of existence, there is little serious alternative to the fundamentals of their legal and political framework. Many are still able to exalt themselves as the country of freedom, and in that exaltation it is the essentially contractual which is being glorified.

While the theoretical foundations of our justice came increasingly to be understood as simply contractual, nevertheless decent legal justice was sustained in our regimes. This can only be comprehended in terms of the intimate and yet ambiguous co-penetration between contractual liberalism and Protestantism in the minds of generations of our people. I am not capable of enucleating the nature of that relation, and it can only be hinted at here. Indeed one can use of that co-penetration the words of one who battled with it in his own being: there is "the sense, in the whole element, of things too numberous, too deep, too obscure, too strange or even simply too beautiful, for any ease of intellectual relation."[18] Perhaps more than any other European country, England's practical flesh and bones have been fed till recently by its remarkable religious traditions. They may not have been the home of much philosophy, but they were a deeply religious people. The more uncouth and less integrated Protestantism of North America has sustained certain forms of justice, at least for those of European origin. Several elementary comments about liberalism and Protestantism are necessary to the understanding of our surviving justice.

To start at the surface: it is clear why the English free church tradition feared established Christian-

theless, even in the immoderation — indeed the fer-
ocity — which has been so manifest in American history, that Protestantism gave a firmer and more
unyielding account of justice to its country's constitutionalism than would have been forthcoming from
any simply contractual account. The continuing
power of American Protestantism in popular life today comes from the fact that it has been a less
thoughtful species of religion than the originating
Protestantism of Europe, and therefore less vulner-
able to modernity. That Protestantism is today above
all pietist. This has given it the strength to continue
even through all the modernising of rural and small
town America. But this pietism has little intellectual
bite compared to the Calvinism it replaced, so that
its direct practical effect on the control of technology
(the central political question) is generally minimal.

All this can be easily said by modern historians.
It is more important to recognise the dependence of
secular liberalism for its moral bite upon the strength
of Protestantism in English-speaking societies. Most
of our history is written by secularists who see the
significant happening as the development of secular
liberalism. They are therefore likely to interpret the
Protestants as passing if useful allies in the realisation of our modern regimes. This allows them to
patronise Protestant superstitions in a friendly man-
ner, as historically helpful in the development of
secularism. To put the ethical relation clearly: if
avoidance of violent death is our highest end (albeit
negative), why should anyone make sacrifices for the
common good which entail that possibility? Why

should anyone choose to be a soldier or policeman, if Lockian contractualism is the truth about justice? Yet such professions are necessary if any approximation to justice and consent are to be maintained. Within a contractualist belief, why should anyone care about the reign of justice more than their life? The believing Protestants provided that necessary moral cement which could not be present for those who were consistently directed by contractualism or utilitarianism or a combination of both. This fundamental political vacuum at the heart of contractual liberalism was hidden for generations by the widespread acceptance of Protestantism. At one and the same time believing Protestants were likely to back their constitutional regimes; yet they backed them without believing that the avoidance of violent death was the highest good, or that justice was to be chosen simply as the most convenient contract.

The word 'dialectic' used about 'history' has had such cruel consequences for so many people that one is loath to use it even loosely. Nevertheless the relation between Protestants and the growing explicitness of secular liberals can be expressed in the political dialectic between them. The more Protestants came to be influenced by the theoretical foundations of the liberalism which they had first accepted for practical reasons, the less were they able to sustain their prime theological belief which had allowed them to support justice in a more than contractual way; therefore they were less able to provide the moral cement which had given vigour to the liberal regimes. The more secular liberals were able to make explicit that their belief in freedom was not simply a matter of political consent, but implied that human beings were the makers of their own laws, the less could they receive from their Protestant supporters that moral force which made their regimes nobler than an individualism which calculated its contracts.

The long history of the gradual secularising of Protestant faith would require a detailed discussion of its relation to the discoveries of modern science and the formulations of modern philosophy. Protestant faith was not only undermined by the objective discoveries of the sciences, but equally by the affirmations concerning humanity in the dominant philosophies. On the scientific side, for example, it was Darwinism which gave Protestant faith its intellectual 'coup de grace' among so many of our bourgeois. On the philosophic side, as 'enlightened' human beings came to express their self-understanding as autonomy—that is, to believe themselves the makers of their own laws—any formulation of Christianity became unthinkable.

This co-penetration of Protestantism and liberalism must not be understood in terms of a simply passive overriding in which Protestantism gradually lost itself. It was a veritable co-penetration in which Protestantism shaped as well as being shaped. In writing of the positive influence of Protestantism on our liberalism, one is forced to touch, however hesitantly, upon the most difficult matter which faces anybody who wishes to understand technology. This is the attempt to articulate that primal western affirmation which stands shaping our whole civilisation, before modern science and technology, before liberalism and capitalism, before our philosophies and theologies. It is present in all of us, and yet hidden to all of us; it originates somewhere and sometime which nobody seems quite to know. Nobody has been able to bring it into the full light of understanding. In all its unfathomedness, the closest I can come to it is the affirmation of human beings as 'will', the content of which word has something to do with how westerners took the Bible as a certain kind of exclusivity. The Calvinist form of Protestantism was a strong breaking forth of that primal and unfathomed affirmation, because 'will' and exclusivity were so central to its theology. Calvinist theological voluntarism made it utterly a modern western theology as distinguished from the theologies of the Platonic world. Hooker saw this with hard practical clarity when he wrote against the Calvinists at the time of their beginnings: "They err who think that of the will of God to do this or that, there is no reason beside his will."[20] In that sense Calvinists were not simply the passive victims of secularisation, but were formulators of it even in their definitions of God and humanity as 'will'. Calvinist secularism is as useful a substantive as secularised Calvinism. Because of their rootedness in what is thought in the word 'will', these Calvinist secularists were particularly open to that definition of will as autonomy. This openness is central to the nemesis of their faith. But in that very nemesis, Calvinism remained a continuing influence in formulating our new 'self-definitions'. An intellectual example from Europe is the fact that thinkers such as Rousseau and Sartre, who were such formulators of human beings as freedom, were both impregnated with Calvinism in their origins. A more important and immediate example is the sheer conflict of competing wills which has characterised the history of American contractualism. "Winning isn't everything; it's all there is."

To turn back from the depths of technology's origins, it may be said simply that the nobility of English-speaking Protestants often lay in what was given them in the word 'freedom', and the consequences of this for the political realm. Nevertheless what was there given them made them prone to take the meaning of the will to be autonomy. But clearly once that Rubicon is crossed, no form of Christianity can consistently stand. As the Protestants accepted the liberalism of autonomous will, they became unable to provide their societies with the public sustenance of uncalculated justice which the contractual account of justice could not provide from itself.

This ambiguous relation between Protestants and secularisation was expressed academically in the influence of Kant among generations of professors — particularly those making the first or second steps away from the pulpit, and finding in the teaching of philosophy an acceptable substitute for preaching. Intellectuals wanted to seem emancipated from Protestantism, even as they were strongly held by it. They liked to see themselves as the friends of freedom and the new technologies, while at the same time they needed to believe that the new society would incorporate the 'absolute moral values' of Protestantism. They could not accept the account of liberalism given in its strictly worldly forms. Kant seemed to tell them how all these needs could be met.

They could be moderns and maintain the 'values' of their past. He seemed to show them how they could believe in freedom as autonomy and in an 'absolute morality' as well. He offered them a Protestantism purified of superstitions and open to progress. A comparison can be drawn between the hopes of these gentle ministers-cum-professors and the more tragic history of the relations between philosophic Jews and German society. The most remarkable of the 'neo-Kantians' was Hermann Cohen, and as late as this century he seems to have been close to identifying the coming of the Messiah with the full realisation of the German liberal state.

In the United States, contractualism was later to be buttressed by other forms of Biblical religion which came with the later immigrants. Both Judaism and Roman Catholicism gave a firmer bite to the political justice lived out under the American constitution than that implied by contractualism. Nevertheless, because the primal formation of that constitutionalism was in the meeting of Protestantism and secular accounts of legality, it cannot be my purpose here to describe how the later immigrant forms of Biblical religion gave force to justice in those institutions, nor to describe how those religions were transformed by existing within English-speaking institutions.[21]

To sum up: the principles of our political and legal institutions did not need to be justified in thought, because they were justified in life. They were lived out by practical people for whom they provided the obvious parameters of any decent society. Anyone who wished to act outside these parameters had rightly to feel or assume shame. They were identified with the coming to be of progressive technological society; they justified and were justified by that coming to be. Through that long period when our bourgeois societies were not only stable at home but increasingly dominant throughout the world, the liberalism could simply be lived in without contemplation. If those who considered themselves political philosophers questioned whether decent rules of justice could be expected to come forth from the foundational affirmation that political relations are simply calculated contracts, they were cushioned from clarity by a long tradition of justice otherwise sustained, and new progressivist hopes. Such intellectuals lived in societies which were enfolded in a sufficiently widespread public religion to produce believers who accepted the liberal state, and yet did not believe that justice was good simply because it was the product of calculated contract. The story has been told many times of how most intellectuals in our societies scorned the fundamental beliefs of the public religion, and yet counted on the continuance of its moral affirmations to serve as the convenient public basis of justice. Clever people generally believed that the foundational principles of justice were chosen conveniences, because of what they had learnt from modern science; nevertheless they could not turn away from a noble content to that justice, because they were enfolded more than they knew in long memories and hopes. They were so enfolded even as they ridiculed the beliefs that kept those memories alive among the less articulate. Intellectual oblivion of eternity could not quickly kill that presence of eternity given in the day to day life of justice. The strength of those very memories held many intellectuals from doubting whether justice is good, and from trying to think why it is good in the light of what we have been told about the whole in modern science. This combination of the public successes of liberalism with these memories and hopes inhibited the thought which asks if justice is more than contractually founded, and whether it can be sustained in the world if it be considered simply a chosen convenience. The very decency and confidence of English-speaking politics was related to the absence of philosophy.

Part IV

English-speaking contractualism lies before us in the majority decision of the U.S. Supreme Court in "Roe vs. Wade". In that decision their highest court ruled that no state has the right to pass legislation which would prevent a citizen from receiving an abortion during the first six months of pregnancy. In that decision one can hear what is being spoken about justice in such modern liberalism more clearly than in academic books which can be so construed as to skim questions when the theory cuts. Theories of justice are inescapably defined in the necessities of legal decision.

Mr. Justice Blackmun begins his majority decision from the principle that the allocation of rights from within the constitution cannot be decided in terms of any knowledge of what is good. Under the constitution, rights are prior to any account of good. Appropriately he quotes Mr. Justice Holmes to this effect, who, more than any judge enucleated the principle that the constitution was based on the acceptance of moral pluralism in society, and that the pluralism was finally justified because we must be properly agnostic about any claim to knowledge of moral good. It was his influence in this fundamental step towards a purely contractual interpretation of their constitution that has above all enshrined him in American liberal hagiography.[22] In the decision, Blackmun interprets rights under the constitution as concerned with the ordering of conflicting claims between 'persons' and legislatures. The members of the legislature may have been persuaded by conceptions of goodness in passing the law in question. However, this is not germane to a judge's responsibility, which is to adjudicate between the rights of the mother and those of the legislature. He adjudicates that the particular law infringes the prior right of the mother to control her own body in the first six months of pregnancy. The individual who would seem to have the greatest interest in the litigation, because his or her life or death is at stake, — namely the particular foetus and indeed all future U.S. foetuses — is said by the judge not to be a party to the litigation. He states that foetuses up to six months are not persons, and as non-persons can have no status in the litigation.

The decision then speaks modern liberalism in its pure contractual form: right prior to good; a foundational contract protecting individual rights; the neutrality of the state concerning moral 'values'; social pluralism supported by and supporting this neutrality. Indeed the decision has been greeted as an example of the nobility of American contractarian institutions and political ideology, because the right of an individual 'person' is defended in the decision against the power of a majority in a legislature.

Nevertheless, however 'liberal' this decision may
seem at the surface, it raises a cup of poison to the
lips of liberalism. The poison is presented in the unthought ontology. In negating the right to existence
for foetuses of less than six months, the judge has
to say what such foetuses are not. They are not persons. But whatever else may be said of mothers and
foetuses, it cannot be denied that they are of the same
species. Pregnant women do not give birth to cats.
Also it is a fact that the foetus is not merely a part
of the mother because it is genetically unique 'ab in-
itio'.[23] In adjudicating for the right of the mother
to choose whether another member of her species
lives or dies, the judge is required to make an ontological distinction between members of the same
species. The mother is a person; the foetus is not.
In deciding what is due in justice to beings of the
same species, he bases such differing dueness on ontology. By calling the distinction ontological I mean
simply that the knowledge which the judge has about
mothers and foetuses is not scientific. To call certain beings 'persons' is not a scientific statement. But
once ontological affirmation is made the basis for
denying the most elementary right of traditional
justice to members of our species, ontological questioning cannot be silenced at this point. Because such
a distinction between members of the same species
has been made, the decision unavoidably opens up
the whole question of what our species is. What is
it about any members of our species which makes
the liberal rights of justice their due? The judge un-
wittingly looses the terrible question: has the long

tradition of liberal right any support in what human beings in fact are? Is this a question that in the modern era can be truthfully answered in the positive? Or does it hand the cup of poison to our liberalism?

This universal question is laid before us in the more particular questions arising from the decision. If foetuses are not persons, why should not the state decide that a week old, a two year old, a seventy or eighty year old is not a person "in the whole sense"? On what basis do we draw the line? Why are the retarded, the criminal or the mentally ill persons? What is it which divides adults from foetuses when the latter have only to cross the bridge of time to catch up with the former? Is the decision saying that what makes an individual a person, and therefore the possessor of rights, is the ability to calculate and assent to contracts? Why are beings so valuable as to require rights, just because they are capable of this calculation? What has happened to the stern demands of equal justice when it sacrifices the right to existence of the inarticulate to the convenience of the articulate? But thought cannot rest in these particular questionings about justice. Through them we are given the fundamental questions. What is it, if anything, about human beings that makes the rights of equal justice their due? What is it about human beings that makes it good that they should have such rights? What is it about any of us that makes our just due fuller than that of stones or flies or chickens or bears? Yet because the decision will not allow the question to remain silent, and yet sounds an ambiguous note as to how it would be answered in terms of our contemporary liberalism, the decision "Commends th' ingredients of our poison'd chalice/ To our own lips."

The need to justify modern liberal justice has been kept in the wings of our English-speaking drama by our power and the strengths of our tradition. In such events as the decision on abortion it begins to walk upon the stage. To put the matter simply: if 'species' is an historical concept and we are a species whose origin and existence can be explained in terms of mechanical necessity and chance, living on a planet which also can be explained in such terms, what requires us to live together according to the principles of equal justice?

For the last centuries a civilisational contradiction has moved our western lives. Our greatest intellectual endeavour — the new co-penetration of 'logos' and 'techne' — affirmed at its heart that in understanding anything we know it as ruled by necessity and chance. This affirmation entailed the elimination of the ancient notion of good from the understanding of anything. At the same time, our day-to-day organisation was in the main directed by a conception of justice formulated in relation to the ancient science, in which the notion of good was essential to the understanding of what is. This civilisational contradiction arose from the attempt of the articulate to hold together what was given them in modern science with a content of justice which had been developed out of an older account of what is.

It must be emphasised that what is at stake in this contradiction is not only the foundations of justice, but more importantly its content. Many academics in many disciplines have described the difference between the ancient and modern conceptions of justice as if it were essentially concerned with differing accounts of the human situation. The view of traditional philosophy and religion is that justice is the overriding order which we do not measure and define, but in terms of which we are measured and defined. The view of modern thought is that justice is a way which we choose in freedom, both individually and publicly, once we have taken our fate into our own hands, and know that we are responsible for what happens. This description of the difference has indeed some use for looking at the history of our race, — useful both to those who welcome and those who deplore the change of view. Nevertheless, concentration on differing 'world views' dims the awareness of what has been at stake concerning justice in recent western history. This dimming takes place in the hardly conscious assumption that while there has been change as to what can be known in philosophy, and change in the prevalence of religious belief among the educated, the basic content of justice in our societies will somehow remain the same. The theoretical differences in 'world views' are turned over to the domain of 'objective' scholarship, and this scholarship is carried out in protected private provinces anaesthetised from any touch with what is happening to the content of justice in the heat of the world. To feel the cutting edge of what is at stake in differing foundations of justice it is necessary to touch those foundations as they are manifested in the very context of justice.

The civilisational contradiction which beset Europe did not arise from the question whether there is justice, but what justice is. Obviously any possible society must have some system of organisation to which the name 'justice' can be given. The contradiction arose because human beings held onto certain aspects of justice which they had found in the ancient account of good, even after they no longer considered that that account of good helped them to understand the way things are. The content of justice was largely given them from its foundations in the Bible (and the classical philosophy which the early Christians thought necessary for understanding the Bible), while they understood the world increasingly in terms of modern technological science.

The desire to have both what was given in the new knowledge, and what was given us about justice in the religious and philosophical traditions, produced many conscious and unconscious attempts at practical and theoretical reconciliations. It is these attempts which make it not inaccurate to call the early centuries of modern liberal Europe the era of secularised Christianity. It is an often repeated platitude that thinkers such as Locke and Rousseau, Kant and Marx were secularised Christians. (Of the last name it is perhaps better to apply the not so different label — secularised Jew.) The reason why an academic such as Professor Rawls has been singled out for attention in this writing is as an example of how late that civilisational contradiction has survived in the sheltered intellectual life of the English-speaking peoples.

Indeed the appropriateness of calling modern contractualism 'secularised Christianity' may be seen in the difference between modern contractualism and the conventionalism of the ancient world. Although the dominant tradition of the ancient world was that justice belonged to the order of things, there was a continuing minority report that justice was simply a man-made convention. But what so startlingly distinguishes this ancient conventionalism from our contractualism is that those who advocated it most clearly also taught that the highest life required retirement from politics. According to Lucretius, the wise man knows that the best life is one of isolation from the dynamism of public life. The dominant contractualist teachers of the modern world have advocated an intense concern with political action. We are called to the supremacy of the practical life in which we must struggle to establish the just contract of equality. When one asks what had been the chief new public intellectual influence between ancient and modern philosophy, the answer must be western Christianity, with its insistence on the primacy of charity and its implications for equality. Modern contractualism's determined political activism relates it to its seedbed in western Christianity. Here again one comes upon that undefined primal affirmation which has been spoken of as concerned with 'will', and which is prior both to technological science and to revolution.

This public contradiction was not first brought into the light of day in the English-speaking world. It was exposed in the writings of Nietzsche. The Germans had received modern ways and thought later than the French or the English and therefore in a form more explicitly divided from the traditional thought. In their philosophy these modern assumptions are most uncompromisingly brought into the light of day. Nietzsche's writings may be singled out as a Rubicon, because more than a hundred years ago he laid down with incomparable lucidity that which is now publicly open: what is given about the whole in technological science cannot be thought together with what is given us concerning justice and truth, reverence and beauty, from our tradition. He does not turn his ridicule primarily against what has been handed to us in Christian revelation and ancient philosophy. What was given there has simply been killed as given, and all that we need to understand is why it was once thought alive. His greatest ridicule is reserved for those who want to maintain a content to 'justice' and 'truth' and 'goodness' out of the corpse that they helped to make a corpse. These are the intellectual democrats who adopt modern thought while picking and choosing among the ethical 'norms' from a dead past. Justice as equality and fairness is that bit of Christian instinct which survives the death of God. As he puts it: "The masses blink and say: 'We are all equal. — Man is but man, before God — we are all equal.' Before God! But now this God has died."

Particularly since Hume, the English moralists had

pointed out that moral rules were useful conventions, but had also assumed that the core of English justice was convenient. Hume's 'monkish virtues'—the parts of the tradition which did not suit the new bourgeoisie—could be shown to be inconvenient; but the heart of the tradition could be maintained and extended in the interests of property and liberty. It could be freed from its justification in terms of eternity, and its rigour could be refurbished by some under the pseudo-eternity of a timeless social contract. But Nietzsche makes clear that if the 'justice' of liberty and equality is only conventional, we may find in the course of an ever changing history that such content is not convenient. He always puts the word 'justice' in quotation marks to show that he does not imply its traditional content, and that its content will vary through the flux of history. The English moralists had not discovered that realm of beings we moderns call 'history', and therefore they did not understand the dominance of historicism over all other statements. Their social contract was indeed a last effort to avoid that dominance, while they increasingly accepted the ways of thought that led ineluctably to historicism. The justice of liberty and equality came forth from rationalists who did not think 'historically'. For whom is such justice convenient when we know that the old rationalism can no longer be thought as 'true'?

However, it is Kant who is singled out by Nietzsche as the clearest expression of this secularised Christianity. Kant's thought is the consummate expression of wanting it both ways. Having understood what is told us about nature in our science, and having understood that we will and make our own history, he turned away from the consequence of those recognitions by enfolding them in the higher affirmation that morality is the one fact of reason, and we are commanded to obedience. According to Nietszche, he limited autonomy by obedience. Because this comfortable anaesthetising from the full consequences of the modern was carried out so brilliantly in the critical system, Nietzsche calls Kant 'the great delayer'. Kant persuaded generations of intellectuals to the happy conclusion that they could keep both the assumptions of technological secularism and the absolutes of the old morality. He allowed them the comfort of continuing to live in the civilisational contradiction of accepting both the will to make one's own life and the old content of justice. He delayed them from knowing that there are no moral facts, but only the moral interpretation of facts, and that these interpretations can be explained as arising from the historical vicissitudes of the instincts. Moral interpretations are what we call our 'values', and these are what our wills impose upon the facts. Because of the brilliance of Kant's delaying tactics, men were held from seeing that justice as equality was a secularised survival of an archaic Christianity, and the absolute commands were simply the man-made 'values' of an era we have transcended.

Nietzsche was the first to make clear the argument that there is no reason to continue to live in that civilisational contradiction. Societies will always need legal systems — call them systems of 'justice' if you like the word. Once we have recognised what we can now will to create through our technology, why should we limit such creation by basing our systems of 'justice' on presuppositions which have been shown to be archaic by the very coming to be of technology? As we move into a society where we will be able to shape not only non-human nature but humanity itself, why should we limit that shaping by doctrines of equal rights which come out of a world view that 'history' has swept away. Does not the production of quality of life require a legal system which gives new range to the rights of the creative and the dynamic? Why should that range be limited by the rights of the weak, the uncreative and the immature? Why should the liberation of women to quality of life be limited by restraints on abortion, particularly when we know that the foetuses are only the product of necessity and chance? Once we have recognised 'history' as the imposing of our wills on an accidental world, does not 'justice' take on a new content?[24]

Against this attack on our 'values', our liberalism so belongs to the flesh and bones of our institutions that it cannot be threatened by something as remote as ontological questioning. The explicit statements of the American constitution guard their system of justice; the British constitution guards the same shape of rights in a less explicit but in a more deeply rooted way. These living forces of allegiance protect the common sense of practical men against the follies of ideologues. Anyway, did not the English-speaking peoples win the wars against the Germans, and win them in the name of liberalism, against the very 'philosophy' that is said to assail that liberalism?

It is also argued that the very greatness of American pluralism, founded upon the contract, is that out of it have come forth continuous religious revivals which produce that moral sustenance necessary to the justice of their society. Is it not a reason for confidence that in the election of 1976 the two candidates competed in allegiance to the traditions of religion, and that there is a renewed interest in religion among the young in the contractual society? Where is the atheism of the right in the United States? Does not the greatness of the American constitution lie in the fact that the general outlines of social cooperation are laid down and maintained by a secular contract, while within those general rules the resources of religious faith can flourish, as long as such faiths do not transgress that general outline? The greatness of the system is that the tolerance of pluralism is combined with the strength of religion. God has not died, as European intellectuals believed; it is just that our differing apprehensions of deity require that the rules of the game are not defined in terms of any of them. The rules of the game are defined in terms of the calculation of worldly self-interest; beyond that, citizens may seek the eternal as they see fit.

Indeed, any sane individual must be glad that we face the unique event of technology within a long legal and political tradition founded on the conception of justice as requiring liberty and equality. When we compare what is happening to multitudes in Asia who live the event of technology from out of ancient and great traditions, but without a comparable sense of individual right, we may count ourselves fortunate to live within our tradition. Asian people often have great advantages over us in the continuing strength of rite; our advantage is in the continuing strength of right. Also our liberalism came from the meeting of Christian tradition with an early form of modern thought, so that our very unthinking confidence in that liberalism has often saved us from modern political plagues which have been devastating in other western societies. At the practical level it is imprudent indeed to speak against the principles, if not the details, of those legal institutions which guard our justice.[25]

Nevertheless, it must be stated that our justice now moves to a lowered content of equal liberty. The chief cause of this is that our justice is being played out within a destiny more comprehensive than itself. A quick name for this is 'technology'. I mean by that word the endeavour which summons forth everything (both human and non-human) to give its reasons, and through the summoning forth of those reasons turns the world into potential raw material, at the disposal of our 'creative' wills.[26] The definition is circular in the sense that what is 'creatively' willed is further expansion of that union of knowing and making given in the linguistic union of 'techne', and 'logos'. Similar but cruder: it has been said that communism and contractual capitalism are predicates of the subject technology. They are ways in which our more comprehensive destiny is lived out. But clearly that technological destiny has its own dynamic conveniences, which easily sweep away our tradition of justice, if the latter gets in the way. The 'creative' in their corporations have been told for many generations that justice is only a convenience. In carrying out the dynamic convenience of technology, why should they not seek a 'justice' which is congruent with those conveniences, and gradually sacrifice the principles of liberty and equality when they conflict with the greater conveniences? What is it about other human beings that should stand in the way of such convenience? The tendency of the majority to get together to insist on a contract guaranteeing justice to them against the 'creative' strong continues indeed to have some limiting power. Its power is, however, itself limited by the fact that the majority of that majority see in the very technological endeavour the hope for their realisation of 'the primary goods', and therefore will often not stand up for the traditional justice when it is inconvenient to that technological endeavour. The majority of the acquiescent think they need the organisers to provide 'the primary goods' more than they need justice.

In such a situation, equality in 'primary goods' for a majority in the heartlands of the empire is likely; but it will be an equality which excludes liberal justice for those who are inconvenient to the 'creative'. It will exclude liberal justice from those who are too weak to enforce contracts—the imprisoned, the mentally unstable, the unborn, the aged, the defeated and sometimes even the morally unconforming. The price for large scale equality under the direction of the 'creative' will be injustice for the very weak. It will be a kind of massive 'equality' in 'primary goods', outside a concern for justice. As Huey Long put it: "When fascism comes to America, it will come in the name of democracy". We move to such a friendly and smooth faced organisation that it will not be recognised for what it is. This lack of recognition is seen clearly when the President of France says he is working for 'an advanced liberal society', just as he is pushing forward laws for the mass destruction of the unborn. What he must mean by liberal is the society organised for the human conveniences which fit the conveniences of technology.

As justice is conceived as the external convenience of contract, it obviously has less and less to do with the good ordering of the inward life. Among the majority in North America, inward life then comes to be ordered around the pursuit of 'primary goods', and/or is taken in terms of a loose popular Freudianism, mediated to the masses by the vast array of social technicians.[27] But it is dangerous to mock socially the fact of contradiction. The modern account of 'the self' is at one with the Nietzschian account. This unity was explicitly avowed by Freud. With its affirmation of the instrumentality of reason, how can it result in a conception of 'justice' similar to that of our tradition? In such a situation, the majorities in the heartlands of the empires may be able to insist on certain external equalities. But as justice is conceived as founded upon contract, and as having nothing to do with the harmony of the inward life, will it be able to sustain the inconveniences of public liberty?

In the western tradition it was believed that the acting out of justice in human relationships was the essential way in which human beings are opened to eternity. Inward and outward justice were considered to be mutually interdependent, in the sense that the inward openness to eternity depended on just practice, and just practice depended on that inward openness to eternity. When public justice is conceived as conventional and contractual, the division between inward and outward is so widened as to prevent any such mutual interdependence. Both openness to eternity and practical justice are weakened in that separation. A. N. Whitehead's shallow dictum that religion is what we do with our solitude aptly expresses that modern separation. It is a destructive half-truth because it makes our solitude narcissistic, and blunts our cutting edge in public justice.

Above all, we do not correctly envisage what is happening when we take our situation simply as new practical difficulties for liberalism, arising from the need to control new technologies, themselves external to that liberalism. Such an understanding of our situation prevents us from becoming aware that our contractual liberalism is not independent of the assumptions of technology in any way that allows it to be the means of transcending those technologies. Our situation is rather that the assumptions underlying contractual liberalism and underlying technology both come from the same matrix of modern thought, from which can arise no reason why the justice of liberty is due to all human beings, irrespective of convenience. In so far as the contemporary systems of liberal practice hold onto the content of free and equal justice, it is because they still rely on older sources which are more and more made unthinkable in the very realisation of technology. When contractual liberals hold within their thought remnants of secularised Christianity or Judaism, these remnants, if made conscious, must be known as unthinkable in terms of what is given in the modern. How, in modern thought, can we find positive answers to the questions: (i) what is it about human beings that makes liberty and equality their due? (ii) why is justice what we are fitted for, when it is not convenient? Why is it our good? The inability of contractual liberals (or indeed Marxists) to answer these questions is the terrifying darkness which has fallen upon modern justice.

Therefore, to those of us who for varying reasons cannot but trust the lineaments of liberal justice, and who somehow have been told that some such justice is due to all human beings and that its living out is, above all, what we are fitted for, — to those of such trust comes the call from that darkness to understand how justice can be thought together with what has been discovered of truth in the coming to be of technology. The great theoretical achievements of the modern era have been quantum physics, the biology of evolutionism, and the modern logic. (All other modern theoretical claims, particularly those in the human sciences, remain as no more than provisional, or even can be known as simply expressions of that oblivion of eternity which has characterised the coming to be of technology.) These are the undoubtable core of truth which has come out of technology, and they cry out to be thought in harmony with the conception of justice as what we are fitted for.

The danger of this darkness is easily belittled by our impoverished use of the word 'thought'. This word is generally used as if it meant an activity necessary to scientists when they come up against a difficulty in their research, or some vague unease beyond calculation when we worry about our existence. Thought is steadfast attention to the whole. The darkness is fearful, because what is at stake is whether anything is good. In the pretechnological era, the central western account of justice clarified the claim that justice is what we are fitted for. It clarified why justice is to render each human being their due, and why what was due to all human beings was "beyond all bargains and without an alternative". That account of justice was written down most carefully and most beautifully in "The Republic" of Plato. For those of us who are Christians, the substance of our belief is that the perfect living out of that justice is unfolded in the Gospels. Why the darkness which enshrouds justice is so dense — even for those who think that what is given in "The Republic" concerning good stands forth as true — is because that truth cannot be thought in unity with what is given in modern science concerning necessity and chance. The darkness is not simply the obscurity of living by that account of justice in the practical tumult of the technological society. Nor is it the impossibility of that account coming to terms with much of the folly of modernity, e.g. the belief that there is a division between 'facts' and 'values'; nor the difficulty of thinking its truth in the presence of historicism. Rather it is that this account has not been thought in unity with the greatest theoretical enterprises of the modern world. This is a great darkness, because it appears certain that rational beings cannot get out of the darkness by accepting either truth and rejecting the other. It is folly simply to return to the ancient account of justice as if the discoveries of the modern science of nature had not been made. It is folly to take the ancient account of justice as simply of antiquarian interest, because without any knowledge of justice as what we are fitted for, we will move into the future with a 'justice' which is terrifying in its potentialities for mad inhumanity of action. The purpose of this writing has been to show the truth of the second of these propositions. In the darkness one should not return as if the discoveries of modern science had not taken place; nor should one give up the question of what it means to say that justice is what we are fitted for; and yet who has been able to think the two together? For those of us who are lucky enough to know that we have been told that justice is what we are fitted for, this is not a practical darkness, but simply a theoretical one. For those who do not believe that they have been so told it is both a practical and theoretical darkness which leads to an ever greater oblivion of eternity.

In the task of lightening the darkness which surrounds justice in our era, we of the English-speaking world have one advantage and one great disadvantage. The advantage is practical: the old and settled legal institutions which still bring forth loyalty from many of the best practical people. The disadvantage is that we have been so long disinterested or even contemptuous of that very thought about the whole which is now required. No other great western tradition has shown such lack of interest in thought, and in the institutions necessary to its possibility. We now pay the price for our long tradition of taking the goods of practical confidence and competence as self-sufficiently the highest goods. In what is left of those secular institutions which should serve the purpose of sustaining such thought — that is, our current institutions of higher learning — there is little encouragement to what might transcend the technically competent, and what is called 'philosophy' is generally little more than analytical competence. Analytical logistics plus historicist scholarship plus even rigourous science do not when added up equal philosophy. When added together they are not capable of producing that thought which is required if justice is to be taken out of the darkness which surrounds it in the technological era. This lack of tradition of thought is one reason why it is improbable that the transcendence of justice over technology will be lived among English-speaking people.

Notes

1. This second point, which would appear to be obvious, has been greatly obscured by recent propagandists for English-speaking liberalism, who in their desire to defend that tradition have denied that other traditions of liberalism have any right to be called 'liberal' at all. At its silliest this kind of writing is to be found in Professor K. Popper's "The Open Society and Its Enemies", particularly in its polemics against Plato and Hegel. It is obviously the proper work of political philosophy to argue, as Montesquieu does so brilliantly in "The Spirit of the Laws", that the modern English polity is a higher regime than the Athenian polis, and that modern philosophers understand the good of liberty in a fuller way than the ancients. Whether Plato understood the good of liberty as well as Locke is a question for serious and difficult argument. But to argue, as Popper does, that Plato and Hegel denied that political liberty was a central human good, and were indeed progenitors of modern totalitarianism, must have required such a casual reading of these two writers that his book can only be considered trivial propaganda. How is it possible to read through "The Apology" or "The Philosophy of Right" and believe that the writers of either did not believe that political liberty

was a central human good? Rather similar arguments
have been advanced by English-speaking liberals against
the tradition of European liberalism which originates with
Rousseau. See for example Bertrand Russell's account of
Rousseau in his "History of Western Philosophy" or J.
L. Talmon's "The Origins of Totalitarian Democracy".
The danger of such writings is that they have encouraged
in our universities a provincial approach towards the
history of political thought, just at a time when our situation required the opposite. For the continuing health of
the liberal tradition, what we least needed was a defen-
sive exclusion of the classical and European traditions
from the canon of liberalism. At a time when massive
technological advance has presented the race with unusual
difficulties concerning political liberty, what was needed
from our academics was an attempt to think through all
that was valuable from the great western traditions which
could help us in dealing with these difficulties. Instead,
what we got from men such as Russell and Popper was
a procrustean affirmation of the self-sufficiency of English
liberalism. To put the matter crudely: in a time of great
intellectual confusion, our crimes at home and abroad
should not prevent us from trying to see what good is
present in English-speaking liberalism, any more than the
crimes of the Soviet Union should prevent us from trying to see what good is present in the tradition that proceeds from Rousseau, or indeed any more than ancient
slavery and imperialism should prevent us looking clearly
at classical political philosophy.

   2. It is of course true that the dilemma arising within
liberalism, because of its imperial as well as its domestic
role, existed as much in the European empires of the nineteenth century as in the American. Indeed, Plato's sustained attacks on Athenian imperialism, and its close rela-

fying themselves with the spread of imperialism; in so far as liberalism became explicitly a universal doctrine of human rights, the liberals had to become critics of their imperialism. A similar dilemma was present from the beginnings of American imperialism, and erupted into immediate political significance over the Vietnam war. The part of F. D. Roosevelt at one and the same time was domestically the liberal part, and abroad established the highest tide of American imperialism. Yet the dominant force in the American protest against that war came from people who protested in the name of liberalism. However ashamed we English-speaking people should be of that war, it should not be forgotten that the strongest anti-imperialist protest in western history occurred in the U.S.A. It may be that the majority of protesters accepted the high consumption due to their imperialism, nevertheless that protest says something about the authenticity of American liberalism.

3. The word 'hierarchy' is still often used as the political opposite to 'equality'. This is bad usage because the subordinations and superordinations of our bureaucracies are not intended to be 'sacred orders' given in the nature of things. There seems to be no current positive word which expresses clearly the opposite of equality. Is this because our liberal language has become increasingly egalitarian, and the lip service we pay to this principle makes it impossible to find accurate words to express what is happening in our institutions?

PART II

4. That Rawls writes within the assumptions of modern liberalism is evident in every page of his writing. Not only does he appeal to Locke, Rousseau and Kant

as his masters, but he covers extensively contemporary English-speaking writing on his subject, not only that of fellow teachers of philosophy, but also that of social scientists interested in theories of justice. All this literature lies within the assumptions of liberalism. To put the matter negatively: Rawls does not give any account of those theoretical positions about morals and politics which in the western world have stood as alternatives to our liberalism. These alternatives can be divided simply into two groups. The first of these is the political philosophy of Plato and Aristotle and the modification of that teaching worked out by their Christian and Jewish followers. This group is temporarily antecedent to our liberalism. The second group is temporarily consequent. It may be quickly typified by calling it the thought dependent upon Marx and that dependent upon Nietzsche. All that need be said about Rawls' approach to classical political philosophy is that in a book on justice there are four times as many references to a certain professor Arrow as there are to Plato. It would appear that for Rawls the classical teaching about moral and political good is simply a dead alternative of only antiquarian interest. Rawls' appeal to Aristotelian psychology is used by him as if that psychology did not live as part of the whole body of Aristotle's teaching. This appeal is therefore not to be taken as an exception to Rawls' disregard of the ancients. As for the great contemporary alternatives to our liberalism, Marx and Marxism are disregarded and Nietzsche is only casually mentioned. For example, the difficulties which historicism presents for moral and political philosophy — difficulties which have engrossed generations of continental European thinkers since Nietzsche — are not discussed. The advantage of this procrustean stance is that it allows Rawls to hold English-speaking liberalism before us for our undivided attention. We swim in a particular bay whose contours we can come to know intimately, and we are never asked to swim out into the ocean the immensities of which can easily overwhelm us. Reading Rawls' book is comparable to reading a contemporary book of Roman Catholic thought in which the issues are presented as the differences of interpretation between Maritain and Teilhard, Rahner and Lonergan. In the same way in Rawls' book we are not diverted from the details at issue within our contemporary liberalism, so that it lies before us to tell us what it is.

5. It might be thought that the names of Hobbes and Rousseau should be added. Rawls finesses the thought of Hobbes in a footnote, saying that there are unspecified 'difficulties' in that thinker. He takes Locke as his master, not Hobbes. Also, why Kant rather than Rousseau? Rousseau was after all the thinker who reformulated contractarian doctrine in the light of his profound criticism of Hobbes' and Locke's account of the origins of human beings. Be that as it may, there are more references to Kant in Rawls' book than to any other thinker. It is well to remember in this connection Kant's continual statements of his debt to Rousseau. English-speaking academics have been apt to regard Kant as a critical epistemologist, to emphasise his debt to Hume and to disregard the fact that his continual tributes to Rousseau are wider than his tribute to Hume. For one of these tributes, see p. 30 of this text. As the subject of this writing is the interdependence between technological reason and reason as political liberalism, it is well to remember that Kant's dedicaton of "The Critique of Pure Reason" to Francis Bacon is combined with his tribute to Rousseau. One partial way of looking at his three "Critiques" is surely as

the attempt to lay before us modern liberalism and technological science as unified in his account of reason. In this sense Rawls is surely right to turn to Kant as his chief master.

6. For a brilliant and extended account of the difference between the state of nature and the original position see A. Bloom's article, "John Rawls vs. The Tradition of Political Philosophy" American Political Science Review, June, 1975.

7. It is indeed little more than journalism to state that in the English-speaking world since 1900 there has been a dominating account of what it is to do philosophy and that the best label to pin upon these complex phenomena is 'analytical'. To become wary of simplifications in this matter, it is only necessary to think of the differences in interest, in method and in doctrine between such disparate practitioners as Russell and Wittgenstein, Quine and Austin; or to think of the subtle intermingling of continental logistics and native English empiricism. Nevertheless it is accurate to say that when youngsters come to study philosophy at our universities they generally meet a curriculum and teachers who require of them certain assumptions as to what that study is. It may be helpful here to remember Walter Rathenau's aphorism: "There are no specialists, there are only vested interests."

8. The underlining is Kant's. "The Groundwork of the Metaphysics of Morals" translated H. J. Paton, Harper's Torchbooks, 1964 p. 61. Also the translation of 'Grundlegung' as 'Groundwork' or elsewhere as 'Fundamental Principles' loses the sense of the enormity of the claim made in the title. Why does Kant have to lay new foundations for the metaphysics of morals? — because all the previous foundations will not do. They will not do be-

cause freedom has not been understood as autonomy, nor the human species understood as the cause of its own development.

9. It is not my business here to describe the holding in unity of these two sides—timeless good and historical will—as it is laid before us through an account of the modern sciences and arts, in the edifice of Kant's three Critiques. However, in an era when oblivion of eternity has almost become the self-definition of many of us, it is necessary to insist on the side of timeless and universal good in Kant's system. Indeed this side is shown with startling clarity by Kant, when despite all the causes which might lead him to propound the philosophy of history, as an essential part of any true philosophical teaching, he turns back from possibility of such an enterprise because it would involve our moral choices depending on knowledge other than the timeless fact of reason itself. See The Critique of Judgement paras. 83 and 84.

10. There is no clearer example of how the vagaries of intellectual history turn inside out the teachings of a great philosopher than the way that Kant's assertion that the morally neutral state is the best state is now generally taken by his liberal successors. For Kant the morally neutral state is advocated on the basis of an egalitarian moral absolutism; today it is often advocated on the basis of moral relativism. The morally neutral state based on sceptical grounds is the strange progeny of the morally neutral state based on absolutist grounds. Perhaps the fate of Kant's doctrine on this matter may be taken to illustrate the fate of inadequate teachings.

11. P. 630 'Fragmente aus dem Nachlasse' in vol. 8, *Immanuel Kant's Sämmtliche Werke*, edited by Gustav Hartenstein, Leipzig, 1968.

12. In describing Rawls account in terms of 'interests'

rather than 'goods', I am not denying that these interests are often unified into the pursuit of what he calls 'life-plans'. I use the word 'interests' to exclude any implication that the word 'good' is used by him in the traditional sense of 'what we are fitted for', or any implication that he believes that we can have knowledge of the highest good for human beings in general. The word 'good' allows Rawls to make use of Aristotle's teaching, through which he attempts to deepen his essentially utilitarian account of happiness by seeming to undergird it with Aristotle's very different account. Commentary on Rawls' version of Aristotle would require the gifts of Dean Swift.

13. I have omitted the words 'consistent with the just saving principle' from Rawls' formulation of his second principle, because they are confusing without a long account of his vague descriptions of his compromises between capitalism and socialism, and of the consequent relation he maintains between economics and politics. Such an account is not essential to my present purposes.

14. The strangest part of Rawls' book is his appeal to Kant as his chief master. The very core of Kant's thought is his sharp division between self-interest and fairness. The moral law of fairness appears to us as categorical command, and therefore simply cuts across the claims of self-interest. It is because of the very great difference between Rawls and Kant on this key issue, and because of Rawls' claim that his theory "is highly Kantian in nature", that I have used the unfriendly metaphor of the shell game about his book.

Part III

15. As in the previous paragraph I have ridiculed Sir Karl Popper's political thought, it is necessary to say that

what is good in his writing is just his trust in the strength of English liberalism to combat the plague of ideology. Foolishly he has combined this trust with an inability to distinguish ideology from philosophy. This is above all evident in his crass writing about Plato.

16. This contempt for Christianity lies at the heart of the division between modern liberalism and the earlier liberties of English history. See for example Churchill's letter to the Times 'On praying for rain'. Both in substance and style this letter might have come from Russell.

17. It is worth repeating that one of the strangest combinations of events in American life was the way that the brutality of their crimes in Vietnam was followed by the very careful protection of domestic rights in the affair of Watergate. To many Americans the victory of their congress and courts over their President seems to have been above all a means of justifying their own self-righteousness, to the end of forgetting what had happened in Vietnam. To understand how that purging worked as an anodyne would require an understanding of the relation between modern liberalism and imperialism.

18. Henry James' preface to "The Aspern Papers". That relation has been illumined by the massive historical scholarship about it in the last generation; but such a relation clearly cannot be fathomed by scholarship. Even Weber or Troeltsch, as they move beyond scholarship towards philosophy, are still unable to catch that self-definition of our wills which arose from the co-penetration. For my comments see *Technology and Empire: Perspectives on North America*, Toronto, 1969.

19. In the fine writing on this matter recently, e.g., the books of Trevor-Roper, Webster, Yates, etc., it is still necessary to single out the early articles of M.B. Foster

as most theoretically illuminating. See Mind 1934-35-36.

20. The Laws of Ecclesiastical Polity, Book I, chap. 2.

21. It is often pointed out that Jewish people remain the most fervent and articulate advocates of our contractualism. Therefore a word must be appended about the relation between Judaism and modern English-speaking regimes. It is obvious why the Jewish community has always welcomed and supported modern liberalism. In western and eastern Europe, Jews had lived for centuries under regimes in which some form of Christianity was the official religion, and under which their survival required both fortitude and patience. As the regimes became secularised, they presented Jews with the possibility of living openly in the civil society. Beyond this obvious fact, it is necessary to understand the deeper question of why Jews have exerted such a formative influence on American society, far beyond their percentage of the population. Perhaps it is that in Judaism worship of God is closely bound together with the existence of a particular historical nation, and that this sense of being a people has given Jews sources of strength when they move out into the impersonal and individualistic public realm consequent on contractualism. Its members have been able to live forcefully in the unblinking public light, because they could retire into the shade of a community not only based on the universality of religion, but on the particularity of nationhood, and these two bound together in a quite unique way. In a society in which contractual relations define more and more human encounters, the Jews have maintained a public force from that given union of worship and nationality, which could only exist sporadically among Christians because of the very nature of Christ's message.

Part IV

22. Blackmun's appeal to Holmes illustrates the uncertainties in current American usage of the words 'liberal' and 'conservative'. His decision about abortion has been put in the 'liberal' column, when it is in fact based on a strict construction of contractualism which is generally put in the 'conservative' column. It is well to remember that Blackmun is a Nixon appointee, and tends in his interpretation of the constitution towards 'strict constructionism', and away from that interpretation according to the changing consensus of a progressing people, which characterised the Warren Court. Nixon consistently advocated over many years that the progressive historicism which dominated the Warren Court should be rectified by the appointment of justices who followed the theory of strict constructionism. This involved that their constitution be conceived as a foundational contract which established certain rights unaffected by the passage of time. But the difference concerning judicial interpretation does not alter the fact that both sides to it appeal to a contractual view of the state, related to the acceptance of the consequences of moral pluralism in society. A foundational contract which is viewed as timeless may seem less oblivious of eternity than an historically developing contract; but in both views justice is considered contractual. Indeed, what is meant in the U.S. by 'conservative' is generally a species of modern 'liberal'.. 'Conservatives' want to hold onto certain consequences of the earlier tradition of our liberalism which more modern 'liberals' are willing to scrap in the interest of the new and the progressive. It is this usage which can be so confusing to people from other countries who may identify 'conservatism' with those who have some memories from before the age

of progress. But the indigenous memories in the U.S. are never from before the age of progress. Thus American 'conservatives' can advocate the most modern technological proposals in the name of 'conservatism'. At the judicial level, this strange usage led certain progressivists to call Mr. Justice Frankfurter a 'conservative' when he became the clearest advocate of strict constructionism on their court.

23. In discussing this case I am not concerned to elucidate the complex question of justice in abortion, whether in individual conduct or positive law. If I were so concerned, I would have to expound these facts of embryology.

24. To put the matter politically: the early public atheism of Europe generally came from 'the left'. Its adherents attacked the traditional religion while taking for granted almost unconsciously that 'the right' would continue to live within its religious allegiances. 'The left' could attack religion partially because it relied on 'the right' having some restraint because of its religion. Philosophers cannot be subsumed under their political effects, but with Nietzsche the atheism of 'the right' enters the western scene. One definition of national socialism is a strange union of the atheisms of 'the right' and of 'the left'.

25. It is well to remember that the greatest contemporary philosopher, Heidegger, published in 1953 "An Introduction to Metaphysics" in which he wrote of National Socialism: "the inner truth and greatness of this movement (namely the encounter between global technology and modern man)". One theoretical part of that encounter was the development of a new jurisprudence, which explicitly distinguished itself from our jurisprudence of rights, because the latter belonged to an era of

plutocratic democracy which needed to be transcended in that encounter. Such arguments must make one extremely careful of the ontological questioning of our jurisprudence, even in its barest contractual form.

26. See M. Heidegger *Der Satz Vom Grund*, Pfullingen, 1957.

27. We are fortunate these days when the social technicians are controlled by something as human as popular Freudianism. Whatever its defects, popular Freudianism is surely superior to the 'new brutalism' of behaviour modification carried out by behaviourist techniques.

Selected Non-Fiction
from
Anansi

tion to democracy, deals with a comparable situation, except for the presence of technology in our day. In England, modern liberalism was above all the creed of the new bourgeois, in that the insistence on political liberties was related to the liberation of dynamic commercial technology, and thus with the expansion of that dynamism around the world. The claim to legal and political freedoms at home was not a claim that could be universally applied abroad to alien races who had to be made the subjects of that commercial technology. This was an even more pressing difficulty for the French, because after the revolution their ideology more explicitly universalised the rights of man. Western principles of right in claiming universality became at one and the same time the basis for anti-imperialism both at home and abroad, yet also a justification for western expansion as the bringing of enlightenment into 'backward' parts of the world. Liberalism as a justification for imperialism can be seen very clearly in the work of Macauley. His account of English history is a panegyric to modern liberalism, with the world-historical good of England's greatness. In India he was the chief instrument in westernising education, and above all for substituting English for Sanskrit in that education. He once said that "All the lore of India is not equal to Aesop's fables". In the intense competition for the world's crassest remark, this one has a high claim. On the other hand, as imperialism developed, the western critique of it came forth largely in the name of liberalism. The antiprogressivist critics of imperialism, such as Cunningham Graham, spoke after all in voices which were not easily understood in modern Europe. Indeed the dilemma became increasingly obvious; in so far as modern liberals put their trust in the development of commerce and technology, they were inevitably identi-